LAW, CRIME AND LAW ENFORCEMENT

LIBEL TOURISM AND FOREIGN LIBEL LAWSUITS

LAW, CRIME AND LAW ENFORCEMENT

Additional books in this series can be found on Nova's website
under the Series tab.

Additional E-books in this series can be found on Nova's website
under the E-books tab.

LAWS AND LEGISLATION

Additional books in this series can be found on Nova's website
under the Series tab.

Additional E-books in this series can be found on Nova's website
under the E-books tab.

LAW, CRIME AND LAW ENFORCEMENT

LIBEL TOURISM AND FOREIGN LIBEL LAWSUITS

AMY J. BROWER
EDITOR

Nova Science Publishers, Inc.
New York

Copyright © 2011 by Nova Science Publishers, Inc.

All rights reserved. No part of this book may be reproduced, stored in a retrieval system or transmitted in any form or by any means: electronic, electrostatic, magnetic, tape, mechanical photocopying, recording or otherwise without the written permission of the Publisher.

For permission to use material from this book please contact us:
Telephone 631-231-7269; Fax 631-231-8175
Web Site: http://www.novapublishers.com

NOTICE TO THE READER

The Publisher has taken reasonable care in the preparation of this book, but makes no expressed or implied warranty of any kind and assumes no responsibility for any errors or omissions. No liability is assumed for incidental or consequential damages in connection with or arising out of information contained in this book. The Publisher shall not be liable for any special, consequential, or exemplary damages resulting, in whole or in part, from the readers' use of, or reliance upon, this material. Any parts of this book based on government reports are so indicated and copyright is claimed for those parts to the extent applicable to compilations of such works.

Independent verification should be sought for any data, advice or recommendations contained in this book. In addition, no responsibility is assumed by the publisher for any injury and/or damage to persons or property arising from any methods, products, instructions, ideas or otherwise contained in this publication.

This publication is designed to provide accurate and authoritative information with regard to the subject matter covered herein. It is sold with the clear understanding that the Publisher is not engaged in rendering legal or any other professional services. If legal or any other expert assistance is required, the services of a competent person should be sought. FROM A DECLARATION OF PARTICIPANTS JOINTLY ADOPTED BY A COMMITTEE OF THE AMERICAN BAR ASSOCIATION AND A COMMITTEE OF PUBLISHERS.

Additional color graphics may be available in the e-book version of this book.

LIBRARY OF CONGRESS CATALOGING-IN-PUBLICATION DATA

Libel tourism and foreign libel lawsuits / editor, Amy J. Brower.
p. cm.
  Includes index.
  ISBN 978-1-61209-148-8 (softcover)
  1. Libel and slander--United States. 2. Conflict of laws--Libel and slander--United States. I. Brower, Amy J.
  KF1266.L53 2010
  346.7303'4--dc22
2010047662

Published by Nova Science Publishers, Inc. † New York

CONTENTS

Preface		**vii**
Chapter 1	"Libel Tourism": Background and Legal Issues *Anna C. Henning and Vivian S. Chu*	**1**
Chapter 2	The SPEECH Act: The Federal Response to "Libel Tourism" *Emily C. Barbour*	**27**
Chapter 3	Testimony of Dr. Rachel Ehrenfeld, Director of the American Center for Democracy, before the Subcommittee on Commercial and Administrative Law, Hearing on "Libel Tourism"	**49**
Chapter 4	Testimony of Bruce D. Brown, Baker & Hostetler LLP, before the Subcommittee on Commercial and Administrative Law, Hearing on "Libel Tourism"	**55**
Chapter 5	Testimony of Laura R. Handman, Davis Wright Tremaine LLP, before the Subcommittee on Commercial and Administrative Law, Hearing on "Libel Tourism"	**71**
Chapter 6	Statement of Professor Linda J. Silberman, Martin Lipton Professor of Law, New York University School of Law, before the Subcommittee on Commercial and Administrative Law, Hearing on "Libel Tourism"	**91**

Contents

Chapter 7 Testimony of Kurt Wimmer, Partner,
Covington & Burling LLP, Hearing
on "Are Foreign Libel Lawsuits Chilling
Americans' First Amendment Rights?" **101**

Chapter Sources **107**

Index **109**

PREFACE

This new book explores recent legislative activity which highlights the phenomenon of "libel tourism," whereby litigants bring libel suits in foreign jurisdictions in order to take advantage of plaintiff-friendly libel laws.

Chapter 1- Recent legislative activity highlights the phenomenon of "libel tourism," whereby litigants bring libel suits in foreign jurisdictions in order to take advantage of plaintiff-friendly libel laws. Suits brought against U.S. citizens in England have been especially prominent.

Chapter 2- The 111th Congress considered several bills addressing "libel tourism," the phenomenon of litigants bringing libel suits in foreign jurisdictions so as to benefit from plaintiff-friendly libel laws. Several U.S. states have also responded to libel tourism by enacting statutes that restrict enforcement of foreign libel judgments. On August 10, 2010, President Barack Obama signed into law the Securing the Protection of our Enduring and Established Constitutional Heritage Act (SPEECH Act), P.L. 111-223, codified at 28 U.S.C. §§ 4101-4105, which bars U.S. courts, both state and federal, from recognizing or enforcing a foreign judgment for defamation unless certain requirements, including consistency with the U.S. Constitution and section 230 of the Communications Act of 1934 (47 U.S.C. § 230), are satisfied.

Chapter 3- This is the testimony of Dr. Rachel Ehrenfeld, Director of the American Center for Democracy, before the Subcommittee on Commercial and Administrative Law, Hearing on "Libel Tourism".

Chapter 4- This is the testimony of Bruce D. Brown, Baker & Hostetler LLP, before the Subcommittee on Commercial and Administrative Law, Hearing on "Libel Tourism".

Chapter 5- This is the testimony of Laura R. Handman, Davis Wright Tremaine LLP, before the Subcommittee on Commercial and Administrative Law, Hearing on "Libel Tourism".

Chapter 6- This is the statement of Professor Linda J. Silberman, Martin Lipton Professor of Law, New York University School of Law, before the Subcommittee on Commercial and Administrative Law, Hearing on "Libel Tourism".

Chapter 7- This is the testimony of Kurt Wimmer, Partner, Covington & Burling LLP, Hearing on "Are Foreign Libel Lawsuits Chilling Americans' First Amendment Rights?"

In: Libel Tourism and Foreign Libel Lawsuits   ISBN: 978-1-61209-148-8
Editor: Amy J. Brower   © 2011 Nova Science Publishers, Inc.

Chapter 1

"LIBEL TOURISM":
BACKGROUND AND LEGAL ISSUES

Anna C. Henning and Vivian S. Chu

SUMMARY

Recent legislative activity highlights the phenomenon of "libel tourism," whereby litigants bring libel suits in foreign jurisdictions in order to take advantage of plaintiff-friendly libel laws. Suits brought against U.S. citizens in England have been especially prominent.

Under the First Amendment to the U.S. Constitution as interpreted by the U.S. Supreme Court in *New York Times v. Sullivan* and its progeny, U.S. courts place the burden of proof on plaintiffs in all defamation cases involving matters of public concern. In addition, a public figure suing in a U.S. court must prove that a defendant acted with "actual malice" (i.e., with knowledge of or with reckless disregard as to the statement's falsity) in order to win a defamation suit. In contrast, in defamation cases brought in England and various other countries, the burden of proof remains with defendants.

Thus, litigants can recover damages in jurisdictions with plaintiff-friendly libel laws as a result of speech that would be protected by the U.S. Constitution in the United States. This situation has prompted concerns regarding a potential "chilling effect," in which authors and publishers will withhold speech that is constitutionally protected, and perhaps even important for national security or a well-functioning democracy, because they fear legal repercussions elsewhere.

Several legislative responses address such concerns. Four states have enacted statutes that restrict their state courts' enforcement of foreign libel judgments. On the federal level, S. 449 and H.R. 1304, introduced during the 111th Congress, propose a federal cause of action which would allow an individual against whom a foreign libel suit was brought to sue, in some circumstances, to (1) bar enforcement of any resulting foreign judgment in U.S. courts, or (2) recover money damages for losses incurred as a result of the foreign libel suit.

The state laws and federal proposals implicate several legal issues. The state laws have prompted calls for a national approach to the recognition of foreign judgments. On the federal level, the legislative debate has prompted questions regarding Congress's authority to act in this area. It has also raised the issue of whether a federal statute should bar enforcement of foreign judgments or take the additional step of establishing a new cause of action enabling suits against foreign libel plaintiffs. The effectiveness of a new cause of action would be shaped by constitutional rules limiting U.S. courts' assertion of personal jurisdiction over foreign defendants. Additionally, international relations concerns might inform some responses to legislative proposals; in particular, there is some possibility that foreign countries could reciprocally decline to enforce U.S. libel judgments or could become less receptive to calls for enforcement of U.S. judgments in legal areas in which U.S. law is relatively friendly to plaintiffs.

In February 2010, a committee of the English House of Commons issued a report recommending reforms to English libel laws. If instituted, such changes might shift the emphasis in the legislative debate to other countries in which libel judgments are obtained more easily than in the United States.

INTRODUCTION

"Libel tourism"[1] is the phenomenon whereby a plaintiff brings a defamation[2] suit in a country with plaintiff-friendly libel laws, even though the parties might have had relatively few contacts with the chosen jurisdiction prior to the suit. As with "forum shopping," the phrase "libel tourism" evokes negative notions regarding a plaintiff's attempt to strategically manipulate legal processes to enhance the likelihood of a favorable outcome. More positively described, a plaintiff's goal might be to find a favorable law under which to obtain redress for a grievance which he perceives as legitimate. Regardless of the characterization, given the increasingly globalized market for publications, some have warned that the libel tourism trend will cause an international lowest common denominator effect for speech, whereby "every writer around the globe [will be subjected] to the restrictions of the most pro-plaintiff libel standards available."[3]

The practice has affected U.S. persons in several suits brought by litigants who wish to avoid the relatively high burden of proof necessary to win defamation claims in the United States. U.S. courts interpret the First Amendment to protect speech that would be considered defamatory under traditional common law and in many other countries. For that reason, U.S. authors and publishers are especially vulnerable to the possibility that a foreign libel judgment will impose penalties for speech that is protected in the author's home country.[4]

Although a committee of the English House of Commons has recommended reforms,[5] England[6] has a long history of providing redress for reputational injuries.[7] Arising from this history, modern English law offers libel plaintiffs a dual advantage: plaintiff-friendly libel laws and a relatively low bar for personal jurisdiction in libel suits. As a result, although England is not the only country with plaintiff-friendly libel laws, English courts have been an especially popular venue for defamation suits.[8]

Because obtaining a judgment and actually receiving money awarded constitute two separate components of a successful lawsuit, winning a judgment in a foreign court does not end the discussion. If a defendant chooses not to appear in a foreign court, the court will typically award a default judgment against the defendant. In such circumstances, plaintiffs in foreign libel suits might involve U.S. courts when they seek to enforce judgments against U.S. defendants because foreign courts typically lack jurisdiction over assets located in the United States. Thus, although foreign libel suits provide context for the issue, legislative proposals have focused on subsequent actions to enforce foreign court judgments in U.S. courts.

KEY CASES AND CALLS FOR LEGISLATIVE ACTION

The most prominent example of the libel tourism trend, and the case most often referenced by bill sponsors and media reports,[9] is the suit brought by a

Saudi billionaire, Sheikh Khalid Bin Mahfouz, against a New York author, Rachel Ehrenfeld, whose book documented his alleged role in financing terrorism.[10] Although the book was published in the United States, an English judge allowed the case to proceed in England because 23 copies of the book were sold through the Internet to English residents.[11] Ehrenfeld did not defend herself in the litigation, and the English court ultimately entered a default judgment against her, awarding more than $200,000 in damages and ordering her to destroy copies of the book and apologize.[12] In response, Ehrenfeld attempted to obtain a judgment from the U.S. District Court for the Southern District of New York declaring Bin Mahfouz' judgment unenforceable. The district court dismissed Ehrenfeld's suit for lack of personal jurisdiction, prompting legislative action, discussed *infra*, in New York State.[13]

A small number of other foreign libel suits have also made headlines. A high-profile suit that has been described as another "striking use of defamation law in an attempt to silence uncomfortable truths" was brought by English historian David Irving against Emory University Professor Deborah Lipstadt after she characterized him as a Holocaust denier.[14] However, the English court in that case ruled in Lipstadt's favor, after finding that her statements regarding Irving were truthful.[15] Other cases have involved defendants from other countries,[16] have settled out of court, or have received less public attention.

A few cases have involved U.S. plaintiffs suing U.S. defendants. An English court dismissed at least one such case on forum *non conveniens* grounds (i.e., because England was an inappropriate forum for litigation given the parties' circumstances) despite finding that it had the requisite ground for jurisdiction.[17] In other cases, English courts have allowed such suits to proceed in England as long as a book or other publication had at least some exposure there.[18]

In response to libel suits against U.S. defendants in foreign courts, some lawmakers and editorial boards have characterized the libel tourism phenomenon as a threat to the United States' strong free-speech protections.[19] A key concern is that foreign libel suits will have a "chilling effect" that extends beyond the harm caused by particular libel cases. The phrase "chilling effect" typically refers to the stifling of protected speech caused by overly broad bases for potential criminal or civil liability for expression.[20] In the libel context, some fear that the possibility of foreign libel suits will stifle speech and publication that is protected by the First Amendment and, in turn, inhibit the exchange of ideas vital to a functioning democracy.[21] Relatedly, proponents of the legislative proposals are troubled by the negative impact of such suits on the fight against terrorism.[22]

In her testimony before the House Judiciary Committee, Ehrenfeld expressed a concern that libel tourism was "limiting [scholars'] ability to write freely about important matters of public policy vital to our national security."[23] Similarly, some have testified about situations in which U.S. authors have been intimidated by a threatened foreign libel suit unless they withdraw publication,[24] and in at least one situation, a publisher removed a book about terrorism funding by two well-known authors from many suppliers after it was sued by Bin Mahfouz in England.[25] Beyond the documented impacts in particular cases, the full extent of the chilling effect caused by foreign libel suits is unclear.

DISTINCTIONS BETWEEN U.S. AND ENGLISH LIBEL LAWS

The U.S. approach to defamation is quite different from the English approach. Although U.S. defamation laws have their origin in and are similar in many ways to the English common law, U.S. defamation laws have evolved differently. The difference is primarily attributable to the Supreme Court's interpretation of the First Amendment to the U.S. Constitution.[26] The U.S. Supreme Court places the burden of proof on plaintiffs, making it more difficult for them to win defamation suits. In some instances, American case law has been called upon in England to aid, and according to some scholars, to "attempt to persuade [English courts] to change the direction of the English law."[27] Likewise, England has developed defenses that make it somewhat more difficult for a public official to succeed in a defamation claim. However, those defenses are not typically available to assist a defendant involved in a libel tourism scenario.

The U.S. Supreme Court established a federal constitutional privilege in defamation law in a landmark First Amendment case, *New York Times v. Sullivan*.[28] The Court held that a public official is prohibited from recovering damages for a defamatory falsehood relating to his official conduct unless he or she can prove with "convincing clarity" that the statement in question was made with "actual malice," defined by the Court as "with knowledge that it was false or with reckless disregard of whether it was false or not."[29] The Court reasoned that this constitutional restriction found its source in the First Amendment, which prohibits any law "abridging freedom of speech or of the press," and which has been applied to the states through the Fourteenth Amendment.[30] The Court further stated that the restriction on recovery is based on a "profound national commitment to the principle that debate on public issues should be uninhibited, robust, and wide-open, and that it may well include vehement, caustic, and sometimes unpleasantly sharp attacks on government and public officials."[31] Furthermore, the Court stated, "It would give public servants an unjustified preference over the public they serve, if critics of official conduct did not have a fair equivalent of the immunity granted to the officials themselves."[32] The Court subsequently extended this constitutional protection to all "public figures."[33]

Defamation liability has also evolved differently in the United States and England with regard to non-public officials and figures. Traditionally, at common law, defamation liability was strict, meaning that a defendant did not have to be aware of the false or defamatory nature of the statement, or even be negligent in failing to ascertain that character. Instead, a plaintiff had to prove only that a statement (1) is defamatory; (2) refers to the claimant; and (3) is communicated to a third party.

Whereas the common law rule still applies in England, U.S. treatment of defamation as a strict liability tort changed with the Supreme Court's decision in *Gertz v. Robert Welch.*[34] In *Gertz*, the Court rejected the English law of strict liability, holding that even a private plaintiff is required to show fault amounting to the defendant's negligence or higher to recover damages.[35] A plaintiff in a U.S. court must prove (1) a false and defamatory communication that concerns another and is (2) an unprivileged publication to a third party; (3) fault that is at least negligence by the publisher; and (4) in certain instances, special damages.

As discussed, unlike the U.S. Supreme Court, English courts have not modified the traditional common law elements that a public official must prove to recover for defamation. Rather, they have allowed a defendant to invoke, as a defense, a qualified or conditional privilege,[36] known as the *Reynolds* Privilege. The *Reynolds* Privilege is a relatively new defense, often referred to as "the test of responsible journalism."[37] In the case of *Reynolds v. Times,*[38] the court considered that statements in the newspaper, which related to the conduct of individuals in public life, should be covered by a qualified privilege. Thus, while Members of Parliament or other public officials need only prove the traditional common law elements of defamation, English courts have made their ability to recover more difficult by giving defendants the *possibility* of claiming that their publications fall under the *Reynolds* Privilege, thus enabling a defendant to avoid liability.

However, the *Reynolds* Privilege seems to be available only to the media, and not authors or others who publish outside the realm of journalism. Furthermore, while the privilege can protect statements made about public officials or figures, in English courts, it is the judge who determines whether the occasion is privileged (i.e., whether the statement rises to the level of being in the public interest), thus allowing a defendant to benefit from use of the defense. In other words, it seems defendants may only invoke the *Reynolds* Privilege if the judge allows them to do so. In the cases of libel tourism litigation, judgments generally have been in plaintiffs' favor, as it appears that defendants who are sued in England have not been able to invoke the *Reynolds* Privilege because they either do not qualify as media, or because their statements are not deemed to be privileged by the judge.

Proposals to reform libel laws in England have garnered attention.[39] A report of a House of Commons committee, printed February 9, 2010, recommends changes such as shifting the burden of proof in some cases; a one-year statute of limitations for libel cases arising from Internet speech; and strengthening the *Reynolds* Privilege.[40] The report explicitly refers to the debate that has taken place in the U.S. Congress as one motivation for the examination of English libel law.[41] It is unclear what specific changes will result from the report.

RECOGNITION OF FOREIGN JUDGMENTS IN U.S. COURTS

State law governs the recognition and enforcement of foreign judgments in U.S. courts. No federal law provides uniform rules, nor is the United States a party to any international agreement regarding treatment of such judgments.[42] Although states generally must recognize judgments from sister states under the Full Faith and Credit clause of the U.S. Constitution, that requirement does not apply to judgments from foreign courts.[43] For that reason, even if one state enacts a law prohibiting its courts from enforcing foreign libel judgments, the judgment might be enforceable in another state where a defendant has assets.

Nonetheless, many states' recognition statutes share identical language, because most are based on one of a few common sources—namely, rules articulated in *Hilton v. Guyot*,[44] a 19th-century U.S. Supreme Court case, or one of two uniform state acts, which in turn draw from *Hilton*. Principles of international comity (i.e., "friendly dealing between nations at peace"[45]) undergird all of these sources. Comity need not be applied reciprocally, and reciprocity has been disregarded as a basis for recognition in some recent U.S. cases. In contrast, countries such as England have adopted a reciprocity-based approach to recognition of foreign judgments.[46] Such countries will generally decline to recognize U.S. judgments if U.S. courts would not recognize a similar judgment rendered by its courts.

In *Hilton*, the Supreme Court explained that international comity is "neither a matter of absolute obligation, on the one hand, nor of mere courtesy and good will, on the other."[47] Rather, "it is the recognition which one nation allows within its territory to the legislative, executive or judicial acts of another nation, having due regard both to international duty and convenience, and to the rights of its own citizens[.]"[48] Under this principle, a foreign judgment should be recognized "where there has been opportunity for a full and fair trial ... under a system of jurisprudence likely to secure an impartial administration of justice ... and there is nothing to show either prejudice in the court, or in the system of laws under which it was sitting, or fraud in procuring the judgment."[49] Although states are not bound by that interpretation,[50] most states have adopted the basic approach from *Hilton* as a matter of statutory or common law.[51]

Two uniform laws[52]—the 1962 Uniform Foreign Money-Judgments Recognition Act and the 2005 Uniform Foreign-Country Money Judgments Recognition Act, which clarifies and updates the 1962 version—provide statutory language which many state legislatures have enacted to codify the basic principles articulated in *Hilton*.[53] More than 30 states have enacted one of the two model laws, in whole or in part. The model acts provide, as a general rule, that "any foreign judgment that is final and conclusive and enforceable where rendered," and in which an award for money damages has been granted or denied, shall be recognized.[54]

However, exceptions apply. Both the common law comity principles and the uniform statutes provide grounds for refusing to recognize foreign judgments. Most relevant is the discretionary public policy exception, which is based on the idea that "no nation is under an unremitting obligation to enforce foreign interests which are fundamentally prejudicial to those of the domestic forum."[55] In states that have enacted the 1962 model act, a court may refuse to recognize a judgment arising from a cause of action or claim for relief that is "repugnant to the public policy of the state."[56] The 2005 version, which only a handful of states have adopted, offers an even broader public policy exception. Under this exception, a state court may refuse to recognize a foreign judgment if the judgment itself, as opposed to the underlying cause of action, is repugnant to the public policy of the state.[57] In addition, it provides a similar ground for nonrecognition if the judgment or cause of action is repugnant to the United States as a whole.[58] By including the foreign judgment itself within the scope of the exception, the act allows a judicial examination of the laws and procedures under which the foreign judgment was rendered. However, although the 2005 act's public policy exception is explicitly broader than the 1962 act's exception, it appears that the change merely incorporates the trend among state courts to interpret the 1962 provision to include judgments, rather than only causes of action, and to include policies of the country as a whole rather than only of the states.[59]

These public policy exceptions have been raised as grounds for nonrecognition in the small number of actions brought in U.S. courts to enforce foreign libel judgments. To date, courts in such cases have declined to enforce foreign libel judgments. To do so, they have relied on public policy exceptions and concluded that foreign libel laws upon which the judgments are based are repugnant to the U.S. Constitution.[60] For example, courts have noted the "substantial" differences between U.S. and English libel laws, "including differences in both substantive law and burdens of proof."[61] Thus, it appears that existing public policy exceptions may bar enforcement of foreign libel judgments in at least some states. However, other states' courts would make their own enforcement decisions.

OVERVIEW OF RULES GOVERNING PERSONAL JURISDICTION

In addition to amending recognition statutes to exclude foreign libel judgments, some legislative responses establish (or would establish) a new cause of action, whereby an individual who has been sued in a foreign court could, in turn, sue the plaintiff in the foreign suit in a U.S. court to establish non-enforcement of a judgment or obtain damages. In order to try such suits, a valid basis must exist for a U.S. court's assertion of personal jurisdiction (i.e., for the exercise of power over a person's rights or liabilities) over plaintiffs in foreign suits.[62]

Constitutional Requirements

A court's assertion of personal jurisdiction over a particular defendant must be both constitutional and statutorily authorized.[63] Thus, even if a state or federal statute expressly authorizes jurisdiction over litigants from foreign libel suits, a court might lack jurisdiction under the due process clauses of the Fifth or Fourteenth Amendments to the U.S. Constitution. In cases brought in state courts or against U.S. defendants, the personal jurisdiction analysis implicates the Fourteenth Amendment due process clause. The Fifth Amendment due process clause applies in cases brought in federal courts against foreign defendants.[64] Pursuant to the federal "long-arm" rule, federal courts' authority to assert personal jurisdiction is generally co-extensive with the jurisdiction of the courts of the state in which they sit, meaning that federal courts must generally analyze personal jurisdiction questions under the relevant state statute and Fourteenth Amendment law.[65] In cases involving foreign defendants, however, federal courts may occasionally assert jurisdiction when the courts of the state in which they sit could not. As discussed *infra*, this occurs when a foreign defendant's contacts with the United States as a whole are constitutionally sufficient even though they would fail to provide a basis for jurisdiction in any individual state.[66]

Although the Fifth Amendment jurisprudence is less developed, the personal jurisdiction analyses appear to be substantially similar under the Fifth and Fourteenth Amendments. In cases interpreting the Fourteenth Amendment due process clause, the Supreme Court has held that personal jurisdiction is constitutional if defendants have had "minimum contacts" in the judicial forum, such that the assertion of jurisdiction "does not offend traditional notions of fair play and substantial justice."[67] In some cases, the defendant must have "purposefully availed" himself of the privilege of carrying out activities in the forum, meaning that a defendant's activities in the forum were such that the defendant should have "reasonably anticipated," rather than merely been able to foresee, the possibility of being haled into court there.[68] The exercise of jurisdiction must also be "reasonable" based on a number of factors.[69] In at least one case, the Court has signaled that "reasonableness" might be a more difficult standard in cases involving foreign defendants, because the cost of defending a suit in the United States would be relatively high for a defendant located abroad.[70]

Similarly, under the Fifth Amendment due process clause, a federal court may exercise jurisdiction if a foreign defendant has "affiliating contacts with the United States sufficient to justify the exercise of personal jurisdiction."[71]

As discussed, under the Federal Rules of Civil Procedure, federal courts may examine the contacts a defendant has with the United States as a whole, rather than contacts with the state in which the court sits, if a defendant has "insufficient contact with any single state to support jurisdiction."[72]

The amount of contacts necessary to meet the constitutional minimum depends, in part, on which type of personal jurisdiction—general or specific—a court asserts. General jurisdiction, which allows a court to exercise jurisdiction over a defendant for any claim, does not require contacts related to the specific claim in the case but instead requires "continuous and systematic" contacts with a forum state (or, if the Federal Rules warrant, with the United States as a whole).[73] Conversely, specific jurisdiction, which limits a court's jurisdiction over a defendant to claims in a particular case, involves no "continuous and systematic" requirement; instead, it requires that a defendant's contacts with the forum "relate to" or "arise out of" the claim at issue in the case.[74] Thus, if a plaintiff in a foreign libel suit had "continuous and systematic" contacts with the United States, then a federal court could assert personal jurisdiction over the foreign plaintiff for any claim. Alternatively, if the plaintiff in the foreign suit had only a small number of contacts with the United States, then the constitutional analysis would likely focus on whether the contacts that arise out of or relate to the foreign libel suit, in particular, were sufficient under the due process clause analysis, including the personal availment and reasonableness inquiries.

For example, merely having a website that could be viewed by people in the United States would be an insufficient basis for jurisdiction because it is not sufficiently targeted toward the United States to meet the "purposeful availment" criteria.[75] In contrast, advertising to solicit business in a state or in the United States as a whole might be sufficient to justify a court's assertion of personal jurisdiction. For example, if a defendant advertised its website to a national audience, personal jurisdiction might be appropriate in any U.S. jurisdiction.[76]

In cases involving tort claims, the Supreme Court has developed an "effects" test, in which the relevant question is whether the harm of the defendant's action was felt in the forum jurisdiction.[77] Interpreted in conjunction with the purposeful availment requirement, the Court requires that the defendant knew that effects would be felt in the forum jurisdiction.[78]

Yahoo!

The federal appellate case most on point regarding U.S. jurisdiction over suits against plaintiffs in foreign libel suits is *Yahoo! Inc. v. La Ligue Contre*

Le Racisme Et L'Antisemitisme.[79] In *Yahoo!*, an *en banc* panel of the U.S. Court of Appeals for the Ninth Circuit determined that courts in California had personal jurisdiction over two French organizations whose only U.S. contacts included actions connected with their libel suit against Yahoo! in France. Specific contacts included (1) a "cease and desist" letter, which the French organizations had mailed to Yahoo! in California; (2) service of process on Yahoo! in California, both to initiate the French lawsuit, and later to effectuate two interim orders by the French court; and (3) Yahoo!'s receipt of court orders from the French lawsuit.[80] After noting that general jurisdiction did not apply, the court imposed a three-pronged test for specific jurisdiction, which essentially incorporates the purposeful availment, reasonableness, and minimum contacts (as apply in specific jurisdiction circumstances) requirements:

> (1) The non-resident defendant must purposefully direct his activities or consummate some transaction with the forum or resident thereof; or perform some act by which he purposefully avails himself of the privilege of conducting activities in the forum, thereby invoking the benefits and protections of its laws;
> (2) the claim must be one which arises out of or relates to the defendant's forum-related activities; and
> (3) the exercise of jurisdiction must comport with fair play and substantial justice, i.e. it must be reasonable.[81]

Under that framework, the court noted that neither the cease and desist letter, nor the service of process, alone, served as a sufficient basis for personal jurisdiction, because both were routine instruments in litigation and not intended to cause harm apart from the litigation.[82] However, applying the effects test to determine whether the purposeful availment prong was satisfied, the court found that the interim court orders—which included an award for money damages—from the French court could have the effect of assessing a "substantial penalty" on Yahoo!, the effects of which would be felt in California. For that reason, the court concluded that personal jurisdiction existed on the basis of Yahoo!'s receipt of the interim court orders in California.[83]

However, the court emphasized that the personal jurisdiction analysis was a "close question."[84] The decision was based on the narrow ground of potential effects of the interim court orders received in California, and other judges on the Ninth Circuit panel strongly disagreed with the court's personal jurisdiction analysis.[85] Furthermore, as discussed, the decision emphasized that

STATE STATUTES

Four states—New York, Illinois, Florida, and California—have enacted statutes addressing the libel tourism phenomenon. The first was New York's Libel Terrorism Protection Act, which makes foreign defamation judgments unenforceable in New York state courts unless a court finds that the foreign country's defamation law provides "at least as much protection for freedom of speech and press" as U.S. law provides.[86] The other state statutes include similar "at least as much protection" language. Under the Illinois and Florida statutes, courts "need not [recognize]" a foreign defamation judgment unless the court "first determines that the defamation law applied in the foreign jurisdiction provides at least as much protection for freedom of speech and the press as provided for by both the United States and [Illinois or Florida] Constitutions."[87] A very similar provision in California provides that a court in that state "is not required to recognize" foreign defamation judgments "unless the court determines that the defamation law applied by the foreign court provided at least as much protection for freedom of speech and the press as provided by both the United States and California Constitutions."[88] These statutes appear to codify, and perhaps expand, the public policy exceptions as applied to libel suits under the states' foreign judgment recognition statutes. Although courts applying state law before the statutes were enacted might have rejected enforcement under the states' existing public policy exceptions,[89] these libel-specific nonrecognition provisions make it more likely that courts will decline to enforce foreign libel judgments—as a matter of court discretion in Illinois, Florida, and California, and under the mandatory statutory provision in New York.

New York, Florida, and California took the additional step of expanding the categories of people over whom courts in those states (and, by implication, federal courts applying state law there) may assert personal jurisdiction (i.e., persons over whom courts may exert power and whose rights and liabilities they may determine). Specifically, New York's statute authorizes personal jurisdiction over "any person who obtains a judgment in a defamation proceeding outside the United States" against (1) a New York resident, (2) a person with assets in New York, or (3) a person who may have to take actions in New York to comply with the judgment.[90] The Florida statute is similar, except that it adds a fourth category of persons or entities who are "amenable to jurisdiction" in Florida.[91] The California statute includes the same four categories but makes it a condition that the foreign judgment was obtained against a California resident or a person or entity amenable to jurisdiction there, and also requires both (1) that the publication at issue was published in California; and (2) the person against whom the judgment might be enforced either has assets in California which may be sought in an enforcement action or may otherwise "have to take actions in California to comply with the foreign-country defamation judgment."[92] These provisions appear to address the dismissal by the U.S. District Court in the *Ehrenfeld* case. Pursuant to the statutes, a court could assert jurisdiction in order to render a declaratory judgment regarding the parties' liabilities and the judgment's enforceability.[93] In other words, the extension of personal jurisdiction permits a cause of action for injunctive relief, whereby courts in those states may declare foreign defamation judgments unenforceable and rule that defendants in the foreign suits have no liability related to the judgments.[94]

LEGISLATIVE PROPOSALS IN THE 111TH CONGRESS

Companion bills, S. 449 and H.R. 1304, both entitled the Free Speech Protection Act of 2009, reintroduce proposed changes to federal law contained in companion bills introduced during the 110th Congress.[95] When introducing the Senate bill, Senator Specter emphasized that the threat of foreign libel suits has caused a "chilling effect" on speech.[96] Like the New York law, the bills would provide both a cause of action for suits by alleged victims of libel tourism against those who had sued them in foreign courts and a basis for personal jurisdiction over these foreign plaintiffs. Specifically, they would establish a cause of action which would apply if two preliminary factors were satisfied: (1) "the writing, utterance, or other speech at issue in the foreign lawsuit does not constitute defamation under United States law"; and (2) "the person or entity which brought the foreign lawsuit serves or causes to be served any documents in connection with such foreign lawsuit on a United States person."

Whereas the bills introduced during the 110th Congress would have purported to authorize personal jurisdiction on the basis of the U.S. defendant's filing (as plaintiff) of a libel suit in a foreign jurisdiction, the bills in the 111th Congress base jurisdiction on service of process on a U.S. person with assets that could be subject to execution. This change appears to be intended to strengthen the likelihood that the jurisdictional basis will be constitutionally valid because it bases jurisdiction on an action (service of process) that takes place in the United States, rather than on an action (filing a suit) that takes place abroad.[97]

The cause of action proposed by S. 449 and H.R. 1304 includes two types of relief—one similar to the relief provided under New York's statute but applicable in all U.S. courts, and a second that goes further. They include (1) injunctive relief declaring the judgment unenforceable in all U.S. courts; and (2) money damages. As introduced, both S. 449 and H.R. 1304 would enable a litigant to bring a suit for money damages in a U.S. court to recover (1) the amount of the foreign judgment; (2) costs incurred as a result of the foreign defamation litigation; and (3) damages from harm "due to decreased opportunities to publish, conduct research, or generate funding." In addition, a court could award "treble damages" (i.e., a court could triple the amount of other damages awarded) if it could be shown, by a preponderance of the evidence, that the foreign suit had been motivated by an intent to "engag[e] in a scheme to suppress First Amendment rights by discouraging publishers or other media not to publish," or by "discouraging" employment or financial support for a certain journalist or other individual.

Questions have arisen regarding whether these affirmative causes of action are necessary to prevent a chilling effect on free speech, particularly in light of U.S. courts' apparent reticence to enforce foreign libel judgments. It has been suggested that a federal statute establishing a "retaliatory" cause of action would be "unprecedented."[98] Nonetheless, proponents of a federal cause of action argue that federal bar to enforcement, alone, is insufficient to prevent a chilling effect.[99]

LEGAL IMPLICATIONS

The state statutes and federal proposals address legitimate concerns regarding the potential negative effects of libel tourism. They also raise a variety of complex legal issues. First, the different state responses have prompted a perceived need for national laws or international treaties[100] to govern the recognition of foreign judgments in state and federal courts, both in the libel area and more generally. Although most states have adopted similar versions of the uniform laws on recognition of foreign judgments, laws specific to the libel context, such as the statutes enacted in the past few years by California, Florida, Illinois, and New York, demonstrate the different approaches states may take to enforcing particular categories of foreign judgments. Such differences could result in different outcomes in enforcement actions brought by foreign litigants in various states. Expressing concern that this lack of uniformity undermines attempts to create coherent international relations strategies, some have argued that the issue of barring or recognizing foreign judgments should be made a matter of national concern.[101]

Second, constitutional requirements might limit the effect of provisions in state laws and the federal companion bills which extend personal jurisdiction over foreign defendants, and of the declaratory judgments rendered pursuant to such jurisdiction. In particular, because it authorizes jurisdiction over defendants who might not direct any activity toward the United States except service of process papers connected with the foreign law suit, some have argued that New York's statute "takes a constitutionally dubious approach to the acquisition of personal jurisdiction."[102] The provisions enacted in Florida and California are more restrictive but might implicate similar concerns. Furthermore, even if courts in those states assert personal jurisdiction and preside over litigation in suits brought to bar the enforcement of foreign libel judgments, the resulting decisions might not be recognized in other states' courts. Under the U.S. Constitution's Full Faith and Credit clause, it would appear that courts in other jurisdictions would be bound to honor decisions regarding litigants' liability in enforcement actions.[103] However, full faith and credit may not be given if a judicial decision was perceived as violating constitutional due process precepts.[104]

Similarly, although the companion bills introduced during the 111th Congress offer a stronger basis for jurisdiction than was proposed by companion bills in the 110th Congress (service of process in the United States versus mere filing of a claim in a foreign court), case law, discussed *supra*, indicates that merely serving process on a U.S. person may be a constitutionally insufficient basis for asserting personal jurisdiction. It is possible that a court would interpret the specific service of process scenario required to trigger jurisdiction in the legislation (service of process on a person with assets in the U.S. that might be subject to execution) as having a harmful effect in the United States, perhaps because the court viewed the service of process in the United States as intended to intimidate a U.S. person. However, it is unclear whether courts would reach that conclusion. Also, orders from foreign courts received by U.S. persons might be sufficient in some cases. Individual cases will likely turn on the number and nature of contacts that particular defendants have with the forum state or, in specified circumstances provided by the Federal Rules of Civil Procedure, with the United States as a whole.

Third, a decision by the United States (or perhaps, even by an individual state) not to enforce particular foreign libel judgments could have negative repercussions on the enforcement of U.S. libel judgments in foreign courts. As discussed, some countries condition recognition of foreign judgments on the foreign country's reciprocal recognition of judgments of the same type. In such countries, U.S. courts' refusal to enforce libel judgments would likely serve as a ground for refusing to enforce libel judgments rendered by U.S. courts.

Finally, some have raised the concern that a basis for nonrecognition of a U.S. cause of action which would provide a penalty for having brought a libel suit in another country could make it difficult for the United States to argue against foreign efforts to undermine enforcement of U.S. judgments in other areas.[105] In some areas of civil tort liability (e.g., antitrust law) the United States has developed particularly plaintiff-friendly laws—the reverse of the United States' relative position in the defamation context. In response, some countries have attempted to undermine the effect of U.S. law in those areas, often by declining to recognize judgments from U.S. courts. In turn, the United States has raised strenuous objections to such efforts. Diplomatic efforts to oppose such efforts by other countries could be compromised if the United States was perceived as employing a similar tactic (i.e., of failing to recognize foreign judgments in a particular area).

CONCLUSION

As a matter of comparative law, U.S. persons, who enjoy relatively strong freedom of speech protections, may experience an undercutting of the rights they enjoy in their home country as a result of a foreign libel suit. In the increasingly globalized world and the post-9/11 era, the libel tourism phenomenon raises legitimate concerns regarding the potential "chilling effect" of foreign libel suits on speech protected by the First Amendment to the U.S. Constitution. Furthermore, although several states have enacted statutes to address the issue, the effect of any one state's action is necessarily limited. In addition, although the extent of the "chilling effect" might be tempered by some courts' apparent willingness to rely on existing state public policy exceptions to decline to recognize foreign libel judgments, not all state recognition laws would produce the same conclusion. Thus, federal statutory responses have been proposed.

However, a few notes of caution might be relevant. First, the effects of creating an express cause of action, as opposed to nonrecognition of foreign judgments, might extend somewhat beyond the response needed to prevent a "chilling effect" in the United States. Although nonrecognition, alone, will not enable U.S. defendants to recover for damages suffered as a result of loss of overseas markets or protect against the need to defend in actions in foreign courts, it would protect speech (and assets) within the United States, at least to some extent. Second, as discussed, a perception that U.S. legislation sought to reform another country's legitimate or even longstanding tort laws could give rise to broader international relations concerns.

As mentioned, a committee of the British House of Commons has recommended significant reforms of English libel laws.[106] However, it is probable that even if enhanced, England's free speech protections would not reach the level of protection extended under the First Amendment to the U.S. Constitution.[107] Additionally, commentators note that England is only one of many countries in which libel suits are more easily won than in the United States.[108] Thus, even if England's libel laws were amended to become less plaintiff-friendly, plaintiffs could still "forum shop" to find other countries with plaintiff-friendly libel laws. These circumstances suggest that domestic federal legislation might be necessary to effectively prevent the negative effect of foreign libel suits on U.S. authors and publishers. On the other hand, the legislative proposals may raise constitutional and foreign relations considerations which might call for caution.

End Notes

[1] The phrase "libel tourism" has appeared in several editorials. *See, e.g.*, David B. Rivkin Jr. and Bruce D. Brown, *Libel Tourism' Threatens Free Speech*, Wall St. J. at A11 (January 10, 2009), and was also the title of a House subcommittee hearing, *Libel Tourism: Hearing Before the Subcomm. on Comm. and Admin. Law of the H. Comm. on the Judiciary*, 111th Cong. (2009). Because several high-profile cases have been brought by alleged supporters of terrorist groups for the supposed purpose of dissuading reporters from exposing their

"Libel Tourism": Background and Legal Issues 19

terrorist connections, the phrase "libel terrorism" has been used in reference to the same phenomenon. *See, e.g.*, Libel Terrorism Protection Act, N.Y. CPLR §§ 302(d), 5304(b)(8).

[2] Defamation is the act of harming a person's reputation by making a false statement to a third person. Libel is defamation within a fixed medium, such as a newspaper, website, sign, etc. For purposes of this chapter, the two terms are used interchangeably.

[3] Avi Bell, Jerusalem Center for Public Affairs, Legacy Heritage Fund, *Libel Tourism: International Forum Shopping for Defamation Claims*, 3 (2008), *http://www.glo* ballawforum.org/UserFiles/puzzle22New(1).pdf.

[4] The United States is not the only jurisdiction to guarantee freedom of expression. For example, the Council of Europe Convention for the Protection of Human Rights and Fundamental Freedoms, which applies in Council of Europe member states, guarantees a freedom of expression right. Council of Europe, *Convention for the Protection of Human Rights and Fundamental Freedoms*, Art. 10. However, many other countries' free speech provisions guarantee more limited protections than the U.S. First Amendment provides. For example, the Council of Europe Convention explicitly states that the right to freedom of expression it provides "may be subject to such formalities, conditions, restrictions or penalties as are prescribed by law and are necessary ... for the protection of the reputation ... of others."

[5] Culture, Media, and Sport Committee, *Press Standards, Privacy and Libel*, 2009-10, H.C. 362-I, II, discussed *infra*.

[6] Although some aspects of English libel law apply throughout the United Kingdom, this chapter refers to "England" because laws may differ in other parts of the United Kingdom, such as Scotland.

[7] *See, e.g.*, *In re Rapier*, 143 U.S. 110 (1892) (noting that libel was a "a well known offence at [English] common law") (citing Lord Campbell in Dugdale's Case, 1 Dearsly Crown Cas. 64, 75; Holt's Laws of Libel, 73).

[8] London has been called the "libel capital" of the world. *See, e.g.*, *Be Reasonable*, London Times (May 19, 2005) at 19 (noting that London has become a libel tourism destination because British laws are "uniquely stacked in [the] favor" of foreign libel plaintiffs).

[9] *See e.g.*, 155 Cong. Rec. S2342 (daily ed. Feb. 13, 2009) (statement of Sen. Specter); Editorial, *Attack of Libel Tourists*, Wash. Post, Feb. 22, 2009 at A22. *See also Libel Tourism: Are English courts stifling free speech around the world?*, Economist (Jan. 8, 2009) ("The best-known [libel tourism] case is that of Rachel Ehrenfeld").

[10] *Bin Mahfouz v. Ehrenfeld*, [2005] EWHC (QB) 1156 (Eng.). Ehrenfeld directs the Center for American Democracy and has written several books documenting links between money streams and terrorist activity. The book at issue was published in 2003 and is entitled "Funding Evil: How Terrorism is Financed and How to Stop It." In testimony before the House Judiciary Committee, Ehrenfeld characterized Bin Mahfouz as a "wealthy and corrupt terror financier." *Hearing on Libel Tourism Before the Subcomm. on Comm. and Admin Law of the H. Comm on the Judiciary*, 111th Cong. (Feb 12, 2009), (statement of Dr. Rachel Ehrenfeld), http://judiciary.house.gov/hearings/pdf/ Ehrenfeld090212.pdf.

[11] *Bin Mahfouz*, [2005] EWHC (QB) 1156 at 22.

[12] *Id*. at 74-75.

[13] 2006 U.S. Dist. LEXIS 23423 (April 25, 2006).

[14] *Irving v. Penguin Books Ltd.*, No. [2000] EWHC (QB) 115.

[15] *Id*. at [13].

[16] For example, a wealthy Ukranian man obtained a default judgment in an English court in 2007 against two Ukranian news organizations. Schillings, Corporate Client Press Releases: "Ukrainian Businessman and Political Leader Files Libel Suit in London" (April 2, 2007), http://www.schillings.co.uk/Display.aspx?MasterId=ebec2217-8ba9-4c82-8e52-23152b660368&NavigationId=330.

[17] *Chadha & Osicom Technologies, Inc. v. Dow Jones & Co.*, [1999] E.M.L.R. 724; [1999] EWCA Civ 1415.

[18] *See* [2000] 2 All ER 986 at 16 (holding that England was an appropriate forum in a suit involving Russian individuals and Forbes Magazine, because some publications had been read in England and the plaintiffs' reputations had been affected there).

[19] *See, e.g.,* Editorial, *Attack of Libel Tourists,* Wash. Post, Feb. 22, 2009 at A22 ("The problem has lightheartedly come to be known as libel tourism, but the damage inflicted on the First Amendment and academic freedom is serious"); Arlen Specter and Joe Lieberman, *Foreign Courts Take Aim at Our Free Speech,* Wall St. J., July 14, 2008, at A15 ("[The United States'] free-flowing marketplace of ideas, protected by our First Amendment ... faces a threat").

[20] Justice Brennan introduced the phrase "chilling effect" in the First Amendment context in a 1965 opinion, *Dombrowski v. Pfister,* 380 U.S. 479, 487 (1965).

[21] *See, e.g.,* 155 Cong. Rec. S2342-43 (daily ed. Feb. 13, 2009) (statement of Sen. Specter) ("[I]t is the chilling effect and the mere threat of litigation that suffices to silence authors; there is no need to try the cases.").

[22] *Id.* (referring to First Amendment freedoms as both "essential to a functioning democracy" and "essential to the fight against terrorism").

[23] *Hearing on Libel Tourism Before the Subcomm. on Comm. and Admin Law of the H. Comm on the Judiciary,* 111th Cong. (Feb 12, 2009), (statement of Dr. Rachel Ehrenfeld).

[24] *See, e.g., Hearing on Libel Tourism Before the Subcomm. on Comm. and Admin Law of the H. Comm on the Judiciary,* 111th Cong. (Feb 12, 2009), (statement of Bruce D. Brown, Partner, Baker & Hostetler LLP) (testifying about the experience of author Humayun Mirza, who wrote a biography of his father, Iskander Mirza, and whose publisher was told that a libel suit would be brought in England if the book went forward). However, Mirza's book, entitled "From Plassey to Pakistan: The Family History of Iskander Mirza, the First President of Pakistan," was published despite the attempted intimidation.

[25] *SeeUp in Smoke,* Wash. Times (Aug. 31, 2007), http://www.washing tontimes. com/ news/2007/ aug/31/up-in-smoke/.

[26] U.S. Const. amend. I ("Congress shall make no law ... abridging the freedom of speech, or of the press.... ").

[27] Clerk and Lindsell on Torts, (Anthony M. Dugdale, et al., 19th ed. 2006) ¶ 23-174 *referring toDerbyshire County Council v. Times Newspapers* [1993] AC 534, which cited *New York Times v. Sullivan.*

[28] 376 U.S. 253 (1964).

[29] *Id.* at 279-80.

[30] *New York Times,* 376 U.S. at 264-65.

[31] *Id.* at 270.

[32] *Id.* at 283. The "immunity granted to officials" refers to the absolute privilege granted to legislators pursuant to the Constitution's speech and debate clause, U.S. Const. art. I, § 6 cl. 1, which if invoked, serves as an absolute bar to recovery, thereby making it difficult for a plaintiff suing a public official to recover for defamation.

[33] *SeeCurtis Publishing Co. v. Butts,* 388 U.S. 130 (1967). The Court has since stated that an individual can be characterized as a public figure or limited public figure in either of two ways: (1) by achieving such pervasive fame or notoriety that he or she becomes a public figure for all purposes and in all contexts; or (2) by voluntarily injecting himself into a particular public controversy and thereby becoming a public figure for a limited range of issues. *Gertz,* 418 U.S. at 351. *See also Harte-Hanks Communications, Inc. v. Cannaughton,* 491 U.S. 657, 666 (1989).

[34] 418 U.S. 323 (1974).

[35] *Id.* at 347.

"Libel Tourism": Background and Legal Issues 21

[36] Qualified, or conditional privilege, is a common law defense in both the U.S. and England, which arises only in specific circumstances. This privilege allows certain types of statements made by a defendant to be immune from claims of defamation.

[37] In order for the defendant to invoke the *Reynolds* Privilege, it is key that the material is in the public interest as determined by the judge, that the defamatory material is justifiable and integral to the public interest, and that the journalist behaved reasonably and responsibly (i.e., the test of responsible journalism). Some factors the court considers are: (1) the source of the information, (2) steps taken to verify the story, and (3) the status of the information. This defense can be defeated upon plaintiff showing that the privileged occasion was misused, i.e., by showing malice.

[38] [2001] 2 AC 127.

[39] *See* Tim Shipman, *MPs: Curb the 'Chilling' Laws Threatening Press Freedom*, DailyMail at 18 (Feb 24, 2010); Howard Gensler, *Some Brit Lawmakers Want Change in Libel Laws*, Phil. Daily News at 36 (Feb 25, 2010); Sarah Lyall, *Britain, Long A Libel Mecca, Reviews Laws*, N.Y. Times at A1 (Dec. 11, 2009).

[40] Culture, Media, and Sport Committee, *Press Standards, Privacy and Libel*, 2009-10, H.C. 362-I, II, http://www.publications.parliament.uk/pa/cm 200910/cmselect/cmcumeds/ 362/ 36202.htm.

[41] *See id.* at paragraph 205 ("[W]e believe that it is more than an embarrassment to our system that legislators in the [United States] should feel the need to take retaliatory steps to protect freedom of speech from what they view as unreasonable attack by judgments in UK courts. The Bills presented in Congress ... clearly demonstrated the depth of hostility to how UK courts are treating 'libel tourism'. It is very regrettable, therefore, that the Government has not sought to discuss the situation with their US counterparts in Washington....").

[42] In January 2009, the United States became a signatory to a convention that would require parties to recognize, with some exceptions, judgments rendered by a court in another signatory country that was designated in a choice of court agreement between litigants. Hague Convention on Choice of Court Agreements (concluded June 30, 2005), *http://w ww.hcch.net/index_en.php?act=conventions.pdf&cid=98*. However, the United States is the first country to sign the Convention, and it is unclear whether other countries will sign it.

[43] U.S. Const. art. IV, § 1 ("Full faith and credit shall be given in each *state* to the public acts, records, and judicial proceedings of every other *state*") (emphasis added).

[44] *Hilton v. Guyot*, 159 U.S. 113 (1895).

[45] *Id.* at 162.

[46] United Kingdom, Foreign Judgments (Reciprocal Enforcement) Act 1933, Chap. 13 23_and_24_Geo_5, pt. 1, § 1.

[47] *Hilton*, 159 U.S. at 163-64.

[48] *Id.*

[49] *Id.* at 202-03. Reciprocity is sometimes included as an additional requirement. In *Hilton*, the Court ultimately declined to enforce a French judgment, despite the judgment's fulfillment of these other requirements, because French courts would not enforce a similar judgment rendered by a U.S. court. *Id.* at 227-228.

[50] The *Hilton* decision established the comity principle for federal courts applying federal common law. Later, in *Erie Railroad Co. v. Tomkins*, 304 U.S. 64 (1938), the Supreme Court held that there is no federal common law. Thus, although the *Hilton* decision no longer binds any U.S. court, its articulation has been incorporated into state common law by multiple states' courts.

[51] *See* Gary B. Born & Peter B. Rutledge, *International Civil Litigation in United States Courts* 1013 (2007).

[52] The uniform laws are model statutes drafted by legal experts under the auspices of the National Conference of Commissioners of Uniform State Laws. States can voluntarily adopt a uniform act as state law.

[53] Nat'l Conf. of Comm. of Uniform State Laws, *Unif. Foreign Money Judgements Recognition Act* (approved in 1962), *http://www.law.upenn.edu/bll/archives/ulc/fnact99/1920_69/uf* mjra62.pdf; Nat'l Conf. of Comm. of Uniform State Laws, *Unif. Foreign-Country Money Judgements Recognition Act* (approved in 2005), http://www.law.upenn.edu/bll/archives/ulc/ufmjra/2005final.pdf. These uniform acts were drafted by the National Conference of Commissioners on Uniform State Laws, a group that drafts uniform state laws in a range of areas. The prefatory note to the 1962 model explained that the model statute "states rules that [had] long been applied by the majority of courts in this country." 1962 Unif. Act at 1.

[54] 1962 Unif. Act at §§ 2, 3; 2005 Unif. Act at §§ 3, 4.

[55] *Laker Airways v. Sabena, Belgian World Airlines*, 731 F.2d 909, 937 (D.C. Cir. 1984). *See also* Born & Rutledge, *International Civil Litigation in United States Courts* at 1061-62.

[56] 1962 Unif. Act at § 4(3).

[57] 2005 Unif. Act at § 4(c)(3).

[58] *Id.*

[59] *See* 2005 Unif. Act at § 4, cmt. 8.

[60] *See, e.g., Telnikoff v. Matusevitch*, 702 A.2d 230, 251 (Md. 1997) (refusing to recognize an English libel judgment because it conflicted with Maryland's public policy concerning freedom of the press and defamation actions), *aff'd* 159 F.3d 636 (D.C.Cir. 1998) (unpublished opinion); *Bachchan v. India Abroad Pubs., Inc.*, 585 N.Y.S.2d 661 (Sup. Ct. N.Y. Cty. 1992) (refusing to recognize a British libel judgment under the public policy exception in New York's foreign judgment recognition statute on ground that British libel law did not accord the protection to free speech and press embodied in U.S. and state constitutions); *Yahoo!, Inc. v. La Ligue Contre le Racisme et L'Anti-semitisme*, 169 F.Supp.2d 1181 (N.D.Cal. 2001) (refusing to enforce an order of a French court, which required an Internet service provider (ISP) to block French citizens' access to Nazi material displayed or offered for sale on the ISP's U.S. site on ground that order's content and viewpoint-based regulation "clearly" would be inconsistent with First Amendment), *rev'd and remanded with instructions to dismiss*, 433 F.3d 1199 (9th Cir. 2006), *cert. denied*, 126 S.Ct. 2332 (2006).

[61] *See, e.g., Soc'y of Lloyd's v. Siemon-Netto*, 457 F.3d 94, 101 (D.D.C. 2006) (distinguishing libel cases, in which the public policy exception validly barred enforcement, from a contract case, in which the legal differences were less substantial).

[62] Although a theoretical question exists regarding the extent to which foreign defendants should be entitled to protection under the due process clause, the Supreme Court seems to have foreclosed this question in the area of personal jurisdiction. *See Asahi Metal Industry Co. v. Superior Court of California, Solano Cty.*, 480 U.S. 102 (1987).

[63] In addition, service of process must have been waived or validly completed.

[64] *See* Fed. Rules Civ. Pro. 4(k), Advisory Comm. Note; *Omni Capital Int'l v. Rudolf Wolff & Co.*, 484 U.S. 97, 103-04 (1987). In cases brought against U.S. defendants, the Fourteenth Amendment analysis governs even in federal courts, because federal procedural rules dictate that federal courts borrow the same analysis as applies in the courts of the state in which it sits to determine whether if is appropriate for courts of that state to exercise jurisdiction over a defendant from another state.

[65] *See* Fed. Rules Civ. Pro. 4(k)(1)(a).

[66] Fed. Rules Civ. Pro. 4(k)(2).

[67] *Int'l Shoe Co. v. Washington*, 326 U.S. 310, 316 (1945) (internal quotations omitted).

[68] *World-Wide Volkswagen Corp. v. Woodson*, 444 U.S. 286, 297 (1980).

[69] Relevant factors the Court has applied, albeit in cases involving U.S. defendants, include, for example, "the forum state's interest in adjudicating the dispute, the plaintiff's interest in obtaining convenient and effective relief." *Id.* In some cases, evidence of purposeful availment might be *prima facie* evidence of reasonableness. *See Burger King Corp. v. Rudzewicz*, 471 U.S. 462, 476-77 (1985).

[70] *Asahi Metal Industry Corp.*, 480 U.S. 102 (1987).

[71] Fed. Rules Civ. Pro. 4(k), Advisory Comm. Note.

[72] *Id.*

[73] *Helicopteros Nacionales de Colombia v. Hall*, 466 U.S. 408, 416 (1984) (internal quotations omitted).

[74] *Id.* at 414 n.8.

[75] *See, e.g., Young v. New Haven Advocate*, 315 F.3d 256, 263 (4th Cir. 2002) (holding that constitutional requirements were unsatisfied where the defendant newspaper had websites with national audiences, because "the fact that the [defendants'] websites could be accessed anywhere ... does not by itself demonstrate that the [defendants were] intentionally directing their website content to" residents in the forum).

[76] *See Bragg v. Linden Research, Inc.*, 487 F.Supp.2d 593 (2007) (holding that personal jurisdiction existed where a website specifically targeted residents in the forum state).

[77] *Calder v. Jones*, 465 U.S. 783 (1984).

[78] *Id.*

[79] 433 F.3d 1199 (9th Cir. 2006) (per curiam).

[80] *Id.* at 1205.

[81] *Id.* at 1205-06.

[82] *Id.* at 1209 ("[W]e do not believe that [the cease and desist] letter is a contact that would, if considered alone, justify the exercise of personal jurisdiction ... [nor do we] regard the service of documents in connection with a suit brought in a foreign court as contacts that by themselves justify the exercise of personal jurisdiction over a foreign litigant in a United States court. If we were to hold that such service were a sufficient basis for jurisdiction, we would be providing a forum-choice tool by which any United States resident sued in a foreign country and served in the United States could bring suit in the United States, regardless of any other basis for jurisdiction.") However, the court signaled that a cease and desist letter targeted to cause harm distinct from the foreign litigation could serve as a basis for personal jurisdiction. *Id.*

[83] *Id.* at 1211.

[84] *Id.*

[85] Dissenters emphasized that the interim orders were "orders of the French court, not acts of the defendants," and argued that "no citizen of any country can safely sue a foreign defendant under the majority's theory of specific jurisdiction because the sought judgment, including [an?] and ordinary money judgment for injury or damages, will have an adverse 'effect' on the defendant's purse.... " *Id.* at 1232-33 (Tashiman, J. concurring in the judgment).

[86] N.Y. CPLR § 5304(b)(8).

[87] 735 ILCS 5/12-621(b)(7); Fla. Stat. § 55.605(2)(h).

[88] Cal. Civ. Pro. Code § 1716(c)(9).

[89] All of the states' foreign judgment recognition statutes—reflecting provisions in the uniform acts—had already provided that foreign judgments need not be recognized if "the cause of action on which the judgment is based is repugnant to the public policy" of the state. 735 ILCS 5/12-621(b)(3); N.Y. CPLR § 5304(b)(4); Cal. Civ. Pro. Code § 1716(c)(3); Fla. Stat. § 555.605(2)(c).

[90] N.Y. CPLR § 302(d).

[91] Fla. Stat. § 55.6055.

[92] Cal. Civ. Pro. Code § 1717(c).

[93] *Id.* A declaratory judgment is a form of equitable relief, whereby a court rules on parties' respective rights or status without ordering any action or money damages.

[94] As discussed *infra*, it is unclear what effect such declaratory judgments in New York courts might have in other states' courts or in federal courts applying state law.

[95] Free Speech Protection Act of 2009, S. 449 and H.R. 1304, 111th Cong. (2009); Free Speech Protection Act of 2008, H.R. 5814 and S. 2977, 110th Cong. (2008).

[96] *See, e.g.,* 155 Cong. Rec. S2342-43 (daily ed. Feb. 13, 2009) (statement of Sen. Specter). His statement cited examples of British publishers who have canceled publication or destroyed books as a result of threats of litigation or threats of litigation.

[97] *See* Sen. Arlen Specter, Sen. Joe Lieberman, and Rep. Peter King, *Confronting Libel Tourism Properly,* Letters to the Editor, Wall St. J. (Jan. 23, 2009) at A14.

[98] *Are Foreign Libel Lawsuits Chilling Americans' First Amendment Rights?: Hearing Before the S. Comm. on the Judiciary,* 111th Cong. (Feb. 23, 2010) (statement of Sen. Leahy).

[99] *See, e.g., id.* (written testimony of Kurt Wimmer, Partner, Covington & Burling), *http://judi*ciary.senate.gov/ hearings/testimony.cfm?id=4414&wit_id=9121 (asserting that because "the very act of rendering a foreign judgment has immediate and damaging effects on [a] publisher or author," a lack of enforcement is insufficient to prevent a chilling effect).

[100] *See, e.g.,* Hague Convention on the Recognition and Enforcement of Foreign Judgments in Civil and Commercial Matters, Feb. 1, 1971, http://hcch.e-vision.nl/index_en.php?act=conventions.pdf&cid=78.

[101] See, e.g., *Libel Tourism: Hearing Before the Subcomm. on Comm. and Admin. Law of the H. Comm. on the Judiciary,* 111th Cong. 2 (2009) (statement of Professor Linda J. Silberman, Martin Lipton Professor of Law, New York University School of Law). Although some might question the extent of Congress's power to regulate the enforcement of foreign judgments in state courts, it is likely that Congress has such authority under its inherent foreign affairs powers, because the recognition and enforcement of foreign judgments naturally relate to foreign affairs and commerce, implicating principles of comity and related foreign relations concerns. The public policy exception incorporated in the comity principle might have similar implications for foreign affairs in that it subjects foreign judgments to domestic scrutiny based upon the content of foreign laws and legal systems vis à vis U.S. laws and legal processes. As discussed above, the free speech and press protections advanced in U.S. public policy and enshrined in the U.S. and state constitutions have been found to be a basis for invoking the public policy exception inherent in the comity principle and included in the uniform foreign judgments acts adopted by many U.S. states. Given that a plaintiff from a foreign libel suit would face potential enforcement actions in courts throughout the United States, Congress might assert a foreign affairs, and perhaps a national, interest in discouraging forum shopping in the United States. Thus, it appears that Congress could enact a uniform rule governing enforcement of foreign judgments—either in the libel tourism area or more generally—in order to ensure predictability in the U.S. posture toward foreign judgments.

[102] David B. Rivkin Jr. and Bruce D. Brown, *'Libel Tourism' Threatens Free Speech,* Wall St. J. at A11 (January 10, 2009).

[103] U.S. Const. Art. IV, Sec. 1 ("Full faith and credit shall be given in each state to the public acts, records, and judicial proceedings of every other state").

[104] *See Underwriters Assur. Co. v. North Carolina Life Ins. Ass'n,* 455 U.S. 691 (1982).

[105] *See, e.g., Libel Tourism: Hearing Before the Subcomm. on Comm. and Admin. Law of the H. Comm. on the Judiciary,* 111th Cong. 2 (2009) (statement of Professor Linda J. Silberman, Martin Lipton Professor of Law, New York University School of Law) ("the attempt to impose the standards of U.S. defamation law on the rest of the world goes too far in many situations, and the reach of [S. 449] fails to give proper respect to the interests of other countries").

[106] Culture, Media and Sport Committee, *Press Standards, Privacy and Libel,* 2009-10, H.C. 362-I, II, http://www.publications.parliament.uk/ pa/cm200910/cmselect/ cmcumeds/ 362/ 36202.htm.

[107] In addition to the substantive differences between U.S. and English libel law, discussed *supra,* defendants in U.S. libel suits gain a procedural advantage, because in *Bose Corp. v. Consumers Union of the United States,* 466 U.S. 485 (1984), the Supreme Court interpreted *New York Times v. Sullivan* as requiring appellate judges to review jury verdicts *de novo*— i.e., to examine the whole record and make their own judgments—in defamation cases in

order to ensure that any libel judgment awarded does not impinge upon a defendant's First Amendment rights.

[108] *See, e.g., Are Foreign Libel Lawsuits Chilling Americans' First Amendment Rights?: Hearing Before the S. Comm. on the Judiciary*, 111th Cong. (Feb. 23, 2010) (statement of Kurt Wimmer, Partner, Covington & Burling) (asserting that even if England were to reform its libel laws, "we would still have an issue in other countries").

In: Libel Tourism and Foreign Libel Lawsuits   ISBN: 978-1-61209-148-8
Editor: Amy J. Brower   © 2011 Nova Science Publishers, Inc.

Chapter 2

THE SPEECH ACT: THE FEDERAL RESPONSE TO "LIBEL TOURISM"

Emily C. Barbour

SUMMARY

The 111th Congress considered several bills addressing "libel tourism," the phenomenon of litigants bringing libel suits in foreign jurisdictions so as to benefit from plaintiff-friendly libel laws. Several U.S. states have also responded to libel tourism by enacting statutes that restrict enforcement of foreign libel judgments. On August 10, 2010, President Barack Obama signed into law the Securing the Protection of our Enduring and Established Constitutional Heritage Act (SPEECH Act), P.L. 111-223, codified at 28 U.S.C. §§ 4101-4105, which bars U.S. courts, both state and federal, from recognizing or enforcing a foreign judgment for defamation unless certain requirements, including consistency with the U.S. Constitution and section 230 of the Communications Act of 1934 (47 U.S.C. § 230), are satisfied.

Although the SPEECH Act does not have an express preemption provision, it appears designed to preempt state laws on foreign libel judgments. It explicitly applies to all "domestic" courts, which it defines to include state courts notwithstanding contrary state law. Moreover, its legislative history suggests that Congress perceived a need for, and understood the SPEECH Act as establishing, a single uniform approach to the problem of foreign libel judgments against U.S. persons.

The SPEECH Act may, however, implicate aspects of international comity. One concern is that foreign countries may opt to decline to enforce U.S. libel judgments or become less receptive to calls for enforcement of U.S. judgments in legal areas in which U.S. law is perceived as relatively friendly to plaintiffs.

BACKGROUND

"Libel tourism"[1] describes the act of bringing a defamation[2] suit in a country with plaintiff-friendly libel laws, even though the parties might have had relatively few contacts with the chosen jurisdiction prior to the suit. Libel tourism, like "forum shopping," may be negatively associated with plaintiffs who attempt to strategically manipulate legal processes to enhance the likelihood of a favorable outcome. However, a "libel tourist" could also be described as a plaintiff seeking favorable law under which to obtain redress for a grievance which he perceives as legitimate. Regardless of the characterization, given the increasingly globalized market for publications, some have warned that the libel tourism trend will cause an international lowest common denominator effect for speech, whereby "every writer around the globe [will be subjected] to the restrictions of the most pro-plaintiff libel standards available."[3]

The practice has affected U.S. persons in several suits brought by litigants who wish to avoid the relatively high burden of proof necessary to win defamation claims in the United States. U.S. courts interpret the First Amendment to protect speech that would be considered defamatory under traditional common law and in many other countries. For that reason, U.S. authors and publishers have been especially vulnerable to the possibility that a foreign libel judgment will impose penalties for speech that is protected in the author's home country.[4]

Although a committee of the English House of Commons has recommended reforms,[5] England[6] has a long history of providing redress for reputational injuries.[7] Modern English law appeals to potential libel tourists primarily because it offers a dual advantage to plaintiffs: plaintiff-friendly libel laws and a relatively low bar for personal jurisdiction in libel suits. As a result, although England is not the only country with plaintiff-friendly libel laws, English courts have been an especially popular venue for defamation suits against U.S. nationals.[8]

Because obtaining a judgment and actually receiving the money awarded constitute two separate components of a successful lawsuit, winning a judgment in a foreign court does not end the discussion. If a defendant chooses not to appear in a foreign court, the court will typically award a default judgment against the defendant. In such circumstances, plaintiffs in foreign libel suits might involve U.S. courts when they seek to enforce judgments against U.S. defendants because foreign courts typically lack jurisdiction over assets located in the United States. Thus, the U.S. response to libel tourism has focused primarily on subsequent actions to recognize or enforce foreign court judgments in U.S. courts. For example, the first federal law on point, the Securing the Protection of our Enduring and Established Constitutional Heritage Act (SPEECH Act), bars U.S. courts, both state and federal, from recognizing or enforcing a foreign judgment for defamation unless certain requirements, including consistency with the U.S. Constitution and section 230 of the Communications Act of 1934 (47 U.S.C. § 230), are satisfied.

OBTAINING DEFAMATION JUDGMENTS OVERSEAS

Distinctions between U.S. and English Libel Laws[9]

U.S. and English defamation laws derive from a common origin, but the latter have evolved into a comparatively plaintiff-friendly approach to defamation that has made England a common destination for libel tourists. Traditionally, at common law, defamation liability under both U.S. and English law was strict, meaning that a defendant did not have to be aware of the false or defamatory nature of the statement, or even be negligent in failing to ascertain that character. Instead, a plaintiff had to prove only that a statement (1) was defamatory; (2) referred to the claimant; and (3) was communicated to a third party. However, this common law liability evolved differently under U.S. and English jurisprudence. Today, the differences between the U.S. and English defamation law is primarily attributable to the U.S. Supreme Court's interpretation of the First Amendment to the U.S. Constitution.[10] Today, U.S. defamation law places the burden of proof on plaintiffs, making it more difficult for them to win.

The U.S. Supreme Court first established a federal constitutional privilege in defamation law in *New York Times v. Sullivan*, a landmark First Amendment case.[11] The Court held that a public official is prohibited from recovering damages for a defamatory falsehood relating to his official conduct unless he or she can prove with "convincing clarity" that the statement in question was made with "actual malice," defined by the Court as "with knowledge that it was false or with reckless disregard of whether it was false or not."[12] The Court derived this constitutional restriction from the text of the First Amendment, which prohibits any law "abridging freedom of speech or of the press," and which has been applied to the states through the Fourteenth Amendment.[13] The Court further stated, "It would give public servants an unjustified preference over the public they serve, if critics of official conduct did not have a fair equivalent of the immunity granted to the officials themselves."[14] The Court subsequently extended this constitutional protection to all "public figures."[15]

A second U.S. Supreme Court case, *Gertz v. Robert Welch*,[16] marked another shift in U.S. defamation law away from the common law approach used by England. In that case, which addressed a defamation suit brought by a *non-public* figure, the Supreme Court rejected the English law of strict liability, holding that even a private plaintiff is required to show fault amounting to the defendant's negligence or higher to recover damages.[17] Accordingly, a plaintiff in a U.S. court must prove (1) a false and defamatory communication that concerns another and is (2) an unprivileged publication to a third party; (3) fault that is at least negligence by the publisher; and (4) in certain instances, special damages.

English courts, on the other hand, have not modified the traditional common law elements that a public official must prove to recover for defamation. Instead, they allow a defendant to invoke, as a defense, a qualified or conditional privilege,[18] known as the *Reynolds* privilege. The *Reynolds* privilege is a relatively new defense, often referred to as "the test of responsible journalism."[19] In the case of *Reynolds v. Times*,[20] the court considered that statements in the newspaper, which related to the conduct of individuals in public life, should be covered by a qualified privilege. Thus, while Members of Parliament or other public officials need only prove the traditional common law elements of defamation, they may be barred from recovery if the defendants are members of the media who can show that the publication in question falls under the *Reynolds* privilege.

The *Reynolds* privilege, however, has limited application. First, it does not appear to be available to authors or others who publish outside the realm of journalism, and, second, the judge decides whether the statement at issue was privileged (i.e., in the public interest), a decision that determines whether the Privilege will apply to the defendant. Defendants in libel tourism suits brought in England have typically not been able to invoke the *Reynolds* privilege because they either do not qualify as media or the judge has not deemed their statements privileged.

In reporting the SPEECH Act out of committee in 2009, the House Committee on the Judiciary noted that British libel law has become more protective of free speech after the House of Lords issued a decision expanding the scope of Britain's *Reynolds* privilege.[21] However, this may have little effect on the majority of libel cases brought against U.S. persons in Britain.[22] Nevertheless, the U.S. response to libel tourism may motivate a re-examination of English libel law,[23] and, indeed, some proposals to reform libel laws in England have already garnered attention.[24] Among the changes that have been recommended are shifting the burden of proof in some cases and creating a one-year statute of limitations for libel cases arising from Internet speech,[25] however future changes cannot be predicted.

Key Cases and the Rationale for Legislative Action

A prominent example of libel tourism[26] is the suit brought by a Saudi billionaire, Sheikh Khalid Bin Mahfouz, against a New York author, Rachel Ehrenfeld, whose book documented his alleged role in financing terrorism.[27] Although the book was published in the United States, an English judge allowed the case to proceed in England because 23 copies of the book were sold through the Internet to English residents.[28] Ehrenfeld did not defend herself in the litigation, and the English court ultimately entered a default judgment against her, awarding more than $200,000 in damages and ordering her to destroy copies of the book and apologize.[29] In subsequent testimony before the House Judiciary Committee, Ehrenfeld expressed a concern that libel tourism was "limiting [scholars'] ability to write freely about important matters of public policy vital to our national security."[30] This prompted concerns among lawmakers about the possible negative impact of libel tourism on the fight against terrorism.[31]

Other cases have involved U.S. plaintiffs suing U.S. defendants. An English court dismissed at least one such case on forum *non conveniens* grounds (i.e., because England was an inappropriate forum for litigation given the parties' circumstances) despite finding that it had the requisite ground for jurisdiction.[32] On some occasions, however, English courts allowed the suits to proceed in England as long as a book or other publication had at least some exposure there.[33]

These suits against U.S. defendants in foreign courts prompted many lawmakers and editorial boards to characterize the libel tourism phenomenon as a threat to the U.S. Constitution's strong free-speech protections.[34] A key concern was that foreign libel suits would have a "chilling effect" on speech because the possibility of civil or criminal liability for expression would deter or stifle speech that is protected within the United States.[35] In turn, without a strong national law in the area, the possibility of foreign libel suits could inhibit the exchange of ideas vital to a functioning democracy.[36]

RECOGNITION OF FOREIGN JUDGMENTS IN U.S. COURTS

Principles Governing Domestic Recognition of Foreign Judgments

Except where preempted by federal law, state law governs the recognition and enforcement of foreign judgments in U.S. courts. No federal law provides uniform rules, nor is the United States a party to any international agreement regarding treatment of such judgments.[37] Although states generally must recognize judgments from sister states under the Full Faith and Credit Clause of the U.S. Constitution, that requirement does not apply to judgments from foreign courts.[38] For that reason, even if one state enacts a law prohibiting its courts from enforcing foreign libel judgments, the judgment might be enforceable in another state where a defendant has assets.

Nonetheless, many states' recognition statutes share identical language, because most are based on one of a few common sources—namely, rules articulated in *Hilton v. Guyot*,[39] a 19th-century U.S. Supreme Court case, or one of two uniform state acts, which in turn draw from *Hilton*. Principles of international comity (i.e., "friendly dealing between nations at peace"[40]) undergird all of these sources. Comity need not be applied reciprocally, and reciprocity has been disregarded as a basis for recognition in some recent U.S. cases.[41] In contrast, countries such as England have adopted a reciprocity-based approach to recognition of foreign judgments.[42] Such countries will generally decline to recognize U.S. judgments if U.S. courts would not recognize a similar judgment rendered by its courts.

In *Hilton*, the Supreme Court explained that international comity is "neither a matter of absolute obligation, on the one hand, nor of mere courtesy and good will, on the other."[43] Rather, "it is the recognition which one nation allows within its territory to the legislative, executive or judicial acts of another nation, having due regard both to international duty and convenience, and to the rights of its own citizens[.]"[44] Under this principle, a foreign judgment should be recognized "where there has been opportunity for a full and fair trial ... under a system of jurisprudence likely to secure an impartial administration of justice ... and there is nothing to show either prejudice in the court, or in the system of laws under which it was sitting, or fraud in procuring the judgment."[45] Although states are not bound by that interpretation,[46] most states have adopted the basic approach from *Hilton* as a matter of statutory or common law.[47]

Two uniform laws[48]—the 1962 Uniform Foreign Money-Judgments Recognition Act and the 2005 Uniform Foreign-Country Money Judgments Recognition Act, which clarifies and updates the 1962 version—provide statutory language which many state legislatures have enacted to codify the basic principles articulated in *Hilton*.[49] More than 30 states have enacted one of the two model laws, in whole or in part. The model acts provide, as a general rule, that "any foreign judgment that is final and conclusive and enforceable where rendered," and in which an award for money damages has been granted or denied, shall be recognized.[50]

However, exceptions apply. Both the common law comity principles and the uniform statutes provide grounds for refusing to recognize foreign judgments. Most relevant is the discretionary public policy exception, which is based on the idea that "no nation is under an unremitting obligation to enforce foreign interests which are fundamentally prejudicial to those of the domestic forum."[51] In states that have enacted the 1962 model act, a court may refuse to recognize a judgment arising from a cause of action or claim for relief that is "repugnant to the public policy of the state."[52] The 2005 version, which only a handful of states have adopted, offers an even broader public policy exception. Under this exception, a state court may refuse to recognize a foreign judgment if the judgment itself, as opposed to the underlying cause of action, is repugnant to the public policy of the state.[53] In addition, it provides a similar ground for nonrecognition if the judgment or cause of action is repugnant to the United States as a whole.[54] By including the foreign judgment itself within the scope of the exception, the act allows a judicial examination of the laws and procedures under which the foreign judgment was rendered. However, although the 2005 act's public policy exception is explicitly broader than the 1962 act's exception, it appears that the change merely incorporates the trend among state courts to interpret the 1962 provision to include judgments, rather than only causes of action, and to include policies of the country as a whole rather than only of the states.[55]

These public policy exceptions have been raised as grounds for nonrecognition in the small number of actions brought in U.S. courts to enforce foreign libel judgments. Even prior to the enactment of the SPEECH Act, courts in such cases generally declined to enforce foreign libel judgments on the basis of the public policy exceptions, concluding that the foreign libel laws upon which the judgments were based are repugnant to the U.S. Constitution.[56]

Nonrecognition Provisions in State Libel Tourism Laws

Although state courts have generally declined to enforce foreign libel judgments, some states enacted statutes addressing the libel tourism phenomenon. The first was New York's Libel Terrorism Protection Act,[57] which makes foreign defamation judgments unenforceable in New York state courts unless a court finds that the foreign country's defamation law provides "at least as much protection for freedom of speech and press" as U.S. law provides.[58] The other state statutes include similar "at least as much protection" language. For example, under the Illinois and Florida statutes, courts "need not [recognize]" a foreign defamation judgment unless the court "first determines that the defamation law applied in the foreign jurisdiction provides at least as much protection for freedom of speech and the press as provided for by both the United States and [Illinois or Florida] Constitutions."[59] In general, these statutes appear to codify, and perhaps expand, the public policy exceptions as applied to libel suits under the states' foreign judgment recognition statutes. Although courts applying state law before the statutes were enacted might have rejected enforcement under the states' existing public policy exceptions,[60] these libel-specific nonrecognition provisions made it more likely that courts in these states would decline to enforce foreign libel judgments.

New York,[61] Florida,[62] and California[63] took the additional step of expanding the categories of people over whom courts in those states (and, by implication, federal courts applying state law there) may assert personal jurisdiction (i.e., persons over whom courts may exert power and whose rights and liabilities they may determine).[64] New York's statute, for example, authorizes personal jurisdiction over "any person who obtains a judgment in a defamation proceeding outside the United States" against (1) a New York resident, (2) a person with assets in New York, or (3) a person who may have to take actions in New York to comply with the judgment.[65] Under all three statutes, the extension of personal jurisdiction permits a cause of action for injunctive relief, whereby courts in those states may declare foreign defamation judgments unenforceable and rule that defendants in the foreign suits have no liability related to the judgments. This change in law would prevent the problems faced by New York author and prominent libel tourism defendant Rachel Ehrenfeld, whose action for a declaratory judgment establishing that Bin Mahfouz's judgment against her was unenforceable in the State of New York was dismissed for lack of personal jurisdiction in 2006.[66]

THE FEDERAL SPEECH ACT

The 111th Congress considered several proposals to address libel tourism,[67] and ultimately passed the Securing the Protection of our Enduring and Established Constitutional Heritage Act (or the "SPEECH Act"),[68] which was signed into law on August 10, 2010.

The SPEECH Act avoided the constitutional questions that accompanied some of the other proposals. For example, S. 449 and H.R. 1304, which were collectively referred to as the Free Speech Protection Act, would have authorized counter-suits and a basis for exercising personal jurisdiction over a person who served documents related to a foreign defamation lawsuit on a U.S. person.[69] Had this approach been adopted, it may have been viewed as authorizing federal courts to exercise personal jurisdiction beyond the boundaries permitted by due process, which requires the defendants to have "minimum contacts" in the judicial forum, such that the court's assertion of jurisdiction over them conforms with traditional notions of fairness.[70] For these reasons, as well as concern for international comity, the House Committee on the Judiciary indicated that this approach would be too aggressive.[71]

Accordingly, the SPEECH Act does not authorize counter-suits against plaintiffs in foreign libel cases. Instead, the SPEECH Act bars U.S. courts from recognizing or enforcing a foreign judgment for defamation unless certain requirements are satisfied.[72] However, advocates of a federal cause of action have argued that, without the threat of a counter-suit, bars on enforcement like the one created by the SPEECH Act are insufficient to prevent a chilling effect on the speech of U.S. persons.[73]

The SPEECH Act prohibits domestic courts from recognizing or enforcing foreign judgments for defamation in any one of three circumstances:

1. When the party opposing recognition or enforcement claims that the judgment is inconsistent with the First Amendment to the Constitution, until and unless the domestic court determines that the judgment is consistent with the First Amendment,
2. When the party opposing recognition or enforcement establishes that the exercise of personal jurisdiction by the foreign court failed to comport with the due process requirements imposed on domestic courts by the U.S. Constitution, or
3. When the foreign judgment is against the provider of an interactive computer service and the party opposing recognition or enforcement claims that the judgment is inconsistent with section 230 of the Communications Act of 1934 (47 U.S.C. § 230) regarding protection for private blocking and screening of offensive material, until and unless the domestic court determines that the judgment is consistent with those provisions.[74]

Moreover, in any of those three circumstances, a U.S. citizen opposing recognition or enforcement of the foreign judgment may bring an action in a federal district court for a declaratory judgment that the foreign judgment is repugnant to the Constitution. The SPEECH Act also permits any action brought in a *state* domestic court to be removed to federal court if there is diversity jurisdiction or one party is a U.S. citizen and the other is either a foreign state or citizen of a foreign state.

The SPEECH Act ensures that a party who appeared in a foreign court rendering a foreign judgment to which the act applies is not deprived of the right to oppose recognition or enforcement of that subsequent judgment. If the party opposing recognition or enforcement of the judgment prevails, the act allows the award of reasonable attorney fees under certain conditions.

Finally, the SPEECH Act appears to preempt state laws related to foreign judgments.[75]

Preemption of State Libel Tourism Laws

The enactment of the federal SPEECH Act may raise questions about its effect in state court proceedings in states with a libel tourism statute. It appears that, to the extent that the federal law places greater restrictions on the nonrecognition of foreign defamation judgments, it will be deemed to conflict and consequently preempt the relevant state law pursuant to the Supremacy Clause of the U.S. Constitution.[76] The Supremacy Clause states that the U.S. Constitution and laws made in pursuance thereof "shall be the supreme law of the land; and the judges in every state shall be bound thereby, any thing in the Constitution or laws of any [s]tate to the contrary notwithstanding."[77]

In general, federal preemption of state law can occur where the federal law has an express provision to that effect, where there is a perceived conflict between the state and federal law, or where the scope of the statute indicates that Congress intended to occupy the field exclusively.[78] The Court has identified two forms of implied conflict preemption: situations in which it is impossible for private parties to comply with both state and federal requirements and situations in which the state law frustrates the purpose of Congress.[79] However, these categories should not be interpreted formalistically[80] because the ultimate touchstone of the preemption analysis is whether, and to what extent, Congress intended, explicitly or implicitly, for the federal law to preempt relevant state law.[81] Like many other federal statutes, the SPEECH Act does not contain an express preemption provision, but its language and legislative history strongly suggest that Congress intended to preempt state laws that conflict with the accomplishment of its purpose.[82]

The primary evidence of Congress's preemptive intent is the explicit language of the SPEECH Act itself. The statute states that its provisions are applicable in all "domestic" courts and defines a "domestic court" to include both state and federal courts, "notwithstanding any other provision of [f]ederal or [s]tate law."[83] In addition, House and the Senate Judiciary Committee reports indicate that Congress believed the SPEECH Act would preempt "[s]tate laws related to foreign judgments."[84] Finally, the importance of ensuring a uniform approach towards foreign libel judgments is also likely to weigh in favor of preemption.[85]

Congressional intent aside, the preemptive effect of the Supremacy Clause can be constrained by other constitutional principles, notably federalism[86] and separation of powers,[87] leading courts to apply a presumption against preemption when the federal law in question appears to interfere with a traditional area of state law.[88] Ultimately, whether such a presumption applies depends primarily on how the federal law is best characterized.[89] In the context of the SPEECH Act, the law's subject matter could be described as state courts and state judicial procedure, subjects that typically fall within the purview of the state legislation.[90] However, the SPEECH Act is perhaps more aptly characterized as a law that ensures uniformity and predictability in the federal and state posture towards foreign libel judgments and, therefore, it will likely be perceived as a law addressing foreign affairs, a subject over which the Congress has the primary lawmaking authority.[91] Accordingly, principles of federalism or separation of powers should not dissuade a court from deeming relevant state law preempted by the SPEECH Act.

Implications for International Comity

A decision by a domestic court pursuant to the SPEECH Act not to enforce particular foreign libel judgments could have negative repercussions on the enforcement of U.S. libel judgments in foreign courts. As discussed, some countries condition recognition of foreign judgments on the foreign country's reciprocal recognition of judgments of the same type. In such countries, U.S. courts' refusal to enforce libel judgments would likely serve as a ground for refusing to enforce libel judgments rendered by state or federal courts in the United States. In particular, in some areas of civil tort liability (e.g., antitrust law) the United States has developed what many believe are exceptionally plaintiff-friendly laws, and some countries have tried to undermine their extraterritorial effect.[92] Any U.S. diplomatic efforts to oppose these efforts by a foreign country, however, could be compromised if the SPEECH Act is perceived as employing a similar tactic.[93]

CONCLUSION

Prior to the enactment of the Securing the Protection of our Enduring and Established Constitutional Heritage Act (SPEECH Act), concern existed over the effect the threat of foreign libel suits was having on the exercise of Americans' freedom of speech rights. Although the U.S. Constitution provides relatively strong freedom of speech protections, it did not prevent courts in countries with a less protective view of speech from entering libel judgments against U.S. persons. The SPEECH Act is intended to address this libel tourism phenomenon and reduce or eliminate the potential "chilling effect" foreign libel suits may have on speech protected by the First Amendment to the U.S. Constitution.

Accordingly, the SPEECH Act prohibits domestic courts from recognizing or enforcing foreign judgments for defamation that are inconsistent with the First Amendment of the Constitution, that were entered by a court that exercised personal jurisdiction in contravention of the due process requirements imposed on U.S. courts by the Constitution, or that were inconsistent with section 230 of the Communications of 1934. Some have argued, however, that, without the threat of a counter-suit, this bar on enforcement will prove insufficient to prevent a chilling effect on the speech of U.S. persons.

There are several state libel tourism laws that predate the enactment of the SPEECH Act; however, the SPEECH Act appears to preempt state lawmaking in this area. Although the SPEECH Act lacks an explicit preemption provision, it applies to all "domestic" courts and defines a "domestic court" to include both state and federal courts, notwithstanding any other provision of state law. Furthermore, the legislative history of the act indicates that Congress believed, one, that the SPEECH Act would preempt state laws related to foreign judgments, and, two, that a uniform national approach towards foreign libel judgments was necessary.

The passage of the SPEECH Act may have implications for international comity. A decision by a state or federal court in the United States not to enforce particular foreign libel judgments could have negative repercussions on the enforcement of U.S. libel or other judgments in foreign courts. This will be particularly true in those countries that condition recognition of foreign judgments on the foreign country's reciprocal recognition of judgments of the same type. Similarly, in some areas, U.S. law is perceived as plaintiff-friendly, and the United States may find its diplomatic efforts to ensure that foreign countries recognize judgments pursuant to these plaintiff-friendly laws are opposed by countries' whose libel judgments are negatively affected by the SPEECH Act.

ACKNOWLEDGMENTS

Portions of this chapter were originally prepared by Anna C. Henning, Legislative Attorney, and Vivian S. Chu, Legislative Attorney, vchu@crs. loc.gov, 7-4576.

Emily C. Barbour

End Notes

[1] The phrase "libel tourism" has appeared in several editorials. *See, e.g.*, David B. Rivkin Jr. and Bruce D. Brown, *'Libel Tourism' Threatens Free Speech*, Wall St. J. at A11 (January 10, 2009), and was also the title of a House subcommittee hearing, *Libel Tourism: Hearing Before the Subcomm. on Comm. and Admin. Law of the H. Comm. on the Judiciary*, 111th Cong. (2009). Because several high-profile cases have been brought by alleged supporters of terrorist groups for the supposed purpose of dissuading reporters from exposing their terrorist connections, the phrase "libel terrorism" has been used in reference to the same phenomenon. *See, e.g.*, Libel Terrorism Protection Act, N.Y. CPLR §§ 302(d), 5304(b)(8).

[2] Defamation is the act of harming a person's reputation by making a false statement to a third person. Libel is defamation within a fixed medium, such as a newspaper, website, sign, etc. For purposes of this chapter, the two terms are used interchangeably.

[3] Avi Bell, Jerusalem Center for Public Affairs, Legacy Heritage Fund, *Libel Tourism: International Forum Shopping for Defamation Claims*, 3 (2008), *http://www.globalla wforum.org/UserFiles/puzzle22New(1).pdf*.

[4] The United States is not the only jurisdiction to guarantee freedom of expression. For example, the Council of Europe Convention for the Protection of Human Rights and Fundamental Freedoms, which applies in Council of Europe member states, guarantees a freedom of expression right. Council of Europe, *Convention for the Protection of Human Rights and Fundamental Freedoms*, Art. 10. However, many other countries' free speech provisions guarantee more limited protections than the U.S. First Amendment provides. For example, the Council of Europe Convention explicitly states that the right to freedom of expression it provides "may be subject to such formalities, conditions, restrictions or penalties as are prescribed by law and are necessary ... for the protection of the reputation ... of others."

[5] Culture, Media, and Sport Committee, *Press Standards, Privacy and Libel*, 2009-10, H.C. 362-I, II, discussed *infra*.

[6] Although some aspects of English libel law apply throughout the United Kingdom, this chapter refers to "England" because laws may differ in other parts of the United Kingdom, such as Scotland.

[7] *See, e.g.*, *In re Rapier*, 143 U.S. 110 (1892) (noting that libel was a "a well known offence at [English] common law") (citing Lord Campbell in Dugdale's Case, 1 Dearsly Crown Cas. 64, 75; Holt's Laws of Libel, 73).

[8] London has been called the "libel capital" of the world. *See, e.g.*, *Be Reasonable*, London Times (May 19, 2005) at 19 (noting that London has become a libel tourism destination because British laws are "uniquely stacked in [the] favor" of foreign libel plaintiffs).

[9] This section of the report was prepared by Vivian Chu, Legislative Attorney, 7-4576.

[10] U.S. Const. amend. I ("Congress shall make no law ... abridging the freedom of speech, or of the press....").

[11] 376 U.S. 253 (1964).

[12] *Id.* at 279-80.

[13] *New York Times*, 376 U.S. at 264-65.

[14] *Id.* at 283. The "immunity granted to officials" refers to the absolute privilege granted to legislators pursuant to the Constitution's speech and debate clause, U.S. Const. art. I, § 6 cl. 1, which if invoked, serves as an absolute bar to recovery, thereby making it difficult for a plaintiff suing a public official to recover for defamation.

[15] *See Curtis Publishing Co. v. Butts*, 388 U.S. 130 (1967). The Court has since stated that an individual can be characterized as a public figure or limited public figure in either of two ways: (1) by achieving such pervasive fame or notoriety that he or she becomes a public figure for all purposes and in all contexts; or (2) by voluntarily injecting himself into a particular public controversy and thereby becoming a public figure for a limited range of

The SPEECH Act: The Federal Response to "Libel Tourism" 41

issues. *Gertz*, 418 U.S. at 351. *See also Harte-Hanks Communications, Inc. v. Cannaughton*, 491 U.S. 657, 666 (1989).

[16] 418 U.S. 323 (1974).

[17] *Id.* at 347.

[18] Qualified, or conditional privilege, is a common law defense that also exists in the United States. *See* RESTATEMENT (SECOND) OF Torts § 593. In general, the doctrine of qualified privilege shields defendants from liability if the communications were made on an occasion or under a set of circumstances that entitles them to protection. *See id. E.g.*, Bochenek v. Walgreen Co., 18 F. Supp. 2d 965, 972 (N.D. Ind. 1998) ("This doctrine protects 'communications made in good faith on any subject matter in which the party making the communication has an interest or in reference to which he has a duty, either public or private, either legal, moral, or social, if made to a person have a corresponding interest or duty.'" (quoting Schrader v. Eli Lilly & Co., 639 N.E.2d 258, 262 (Ind. 1994)). A claim of qualified privilege is defeated upon a showing that, in making the statement, the speaker abused the privilege because he either knew that the statement was false or otherwise acted with reckless disregard for the truth. RESTATEMENT (SECOND) OF Torts § 600. *E.g.*, Ewald v. Wal-Mart Stores, 139 F.3d 619, 622-23 (8th Cir. 1998) (finding that an employer's statements to the plaintiff-employee, as well as to other employees, concerning the reason for his discharge were entitled to qualified privilege and there was no evidence of fault to defeat the application of the privilege); *Bochenek*, 18 F. Supp. at 972-74 (finding that plaintiff-employee failed to substantiate her claim that the allegedly defamatory statements about her discharge were made with malice and thereby failed to defeat the application of qualified privilege).

[19] In order for the defendant to invoke the *Reynolds* Privilege, it is key that the material is in the public interest as determined by the judge, that the defamatory material is justifiable and integral to the public interest, and that the journalist behaved reasonably and responsibly (i.e., the test of responsible journalism). Some factors the court considers are (1) the source of the information, (2) steps taken to verify the story, and (3) the status of the information. This defense can be defeated upon plaintiff showing that the privileged occasion was misused (i.e., by showing malice).

[20] [2001] 2 AC 127 (H.L.) (appeal taken from Eng.).

[21] H.Rept. 111-154, at 7 (2009) (referring to Jameel v. Wall St. J. Europe S.P.R.L. [2006] UKHL 44, [2007] 1 A.C. 359 (appeal taken from Britain) (H.L.))

[22] *See id.* ("[T]he Lords' decision is not as speech-protective as *New York Times v. Sullivan* ...").

[23] Culture, Media, and Sport Committee, *Press Standards, Privacy and Libel*, 2009-10, H.C. 362-I, II, at ¶ 205, http://www.publications.parliament.uk/pa/cm 200910/cmselect/cmcumeds/ 362/36202.htm. *See id.* at paragraph 205 ("[W]e believe that it is more than an embarrassment to our system that legislators in the [United States] should feel the need to take retaliatory steps to protect freedom of speech from what they view as unreasonable attack by judgments in UK courts. The Bills presented in Congress ... clearly demonstrated the depth of hostility to how UK courts are treating 'libel tourism.' It is very regrettable, therefore, that the Government has not sought to discuss the situation with their US counterparts in Washington....").

[24] *See* Tim Shipman, *MPs: Curb the 'Chilling' Laws Threatening Press Freedom*, DAILY MAIL at 18 (Feb. 24, 2010); Howard Gensler, *Some Brit Lawmakers Want Change in Libel Laws*, Phil. Daily News at 36 (Feb. 25, 2010); Sarah Lyall, *Britain, Long A Libel Mecca, Reviews Laws*, N.Y. TIMES at A1 (Dec. 11, 2009).

[25] Culture, Media, and Sport Committee, *supra* note 23.

[26] *See, e.g.*, 155 Cong. Rec. S2342 (daily ed. Feb. 13, 2009) (statement of Sen. Specter); Editorial, *Attack of Libel Tourists*, Wash. Post, Feb. 22, 2009 at A22. *See also Libel Tourism: Are English courts stifling free speech around the world?*, Economist (Jan. 8, 2009) ("The best-known [libel tourism] case is that of Rachel Ehrenfeld").

42 Emily C. Barbour

[27] *Bin Mahfouz v. Ehrenfeld*, [2005] EWHC 1156 (QB) (Eng.). Ehrenfeld directs the Center for American Democracy and has written several books documenting links between money streams and terrorist activity. The book at issue was published in 2003 and is entitled "Funding Evil: How Terrorism is Financed and How to Stop It." In testimony before the House Judiciary Committee, Ehrenfeld characterized Bin Mahfouz as a "wealthy and corrupt terror financier." *Hearing on Libel Tourism Before the Subcomm. on Comm. and Admin. Law of the H. Comm. on the Judiciary*, 111th Cong. (Feb 12, 2009), (statement of Dr. Rachel Ehrenfeld), http://judiciary.house.gov/hearings/pdf/ Ehrenfeld090212.pdf.

[28] *Bin Mahfouz*, [2005] EWHC (QB) 1156 at 22.

[29] *Id.* at 74-75. In response, Ehrenfeld attempted to obtain a judgment from the U.S. District Court for the Southern District of New York declaring Bin Mahfouz's judgment unenforceable. The district court dismissed Ehrenfeld's suit for lack of personal jurisdiction, prompting legislative action, discussed *infra*, in New York State. 2006 U.S. Dist. LEXIS 23423 (April 25, 2006).

[30] *Hearing on Libel Tourism Before the Subcomm. on Comm. and Admin Law of the H. Comm. on the Judiciary*, 111th Cong. (Feb 12, 2009), (statement of Dr. Rachel Ehrenfeld).

[31] *Id.* (referring to First Amendment freedoms as both "essential to a functioning democracy" and "essential to the fight against terrorism").

[32] *Chadha & Osicom Technologies, Inc. v. Dow Jones & Co.*, [1999] E.M.L.R. 724; [1999] EWCA Civ 1415.

[33] *See* [2000] 2 All ER 986 at 16 (holding that England was an appropriate forum in a suit involving Russian individuals and Forbes Magazine, because some publications had been read in England and the plaintiffs' reputations had been affected there).

[34] *See, e.g.*, Editorial, *Attack of Libel Tourists*, Wash. Post, Feb. 22, 2009 at A22 ("The problem has lightheartedly come to be known as libel tourism, but the damage inflicted on the First Amendment and academic freedom is serious"); Arlen Specter and Joe Lieberman, *Foreign Courts Take Aim at Our Free Speech*, Wall St. J., July 14, 2008, at A15 ("[The United States'] free-flowing marketplace of ideas, protected by our First Amendment ... faces a threat").

[35] Justice Brennan introduced the phrase "chilling effect" in the First Amendment context in a 1965 opinion, *Dombrowski v. Pfister*, 380 U.S. 479, 487 (1965).

[36] *See, e.g.*, 155 Cong. Rec. S2342-43 (daily ed. Feb. 13, 2009) (statement of Sen. Specter) ("[I]t is the chilling effect and the mere threat of litigation that suffices to silence authors; there is no need to try the cases.").

[37] In January 2009, the United States became a signatory to a the Hague Convention on Choice of Court Agreements, which requires its parties to recognize, with some exceptions, judgments rendered by a court in another signatory country that was designated in a choice of court agreement between litigants. Hague Convention on Choice of Court Agreements, June 30, 2005, 44 I.L.M. 1294, *available at http://www.hcch.net/index_en.php?act=conventions.pd f& cid=98*. Although 29 countries, including the United Kingdom under the auspices of the European Union, had signed the Convention as of August 17, 2010, the Convention will not enter force until at least two countries deposit instruments of ratification or accession with the Ministry of Foreign Affairs of the Kingdom of the Netherlands, the designated depositary of the Convention. *Id.* at Arts. 27, 31. To see a list of parties and signatories as of August 17, 2010, visit *http://www.hcch.net/uploa*d/statmtrx_e.pdf.

[38] U.S. Const. art. IV, § 1 ("Full faith and credit shall be given in each *state* to the public acts, records, and judicial proceedings of every other *state*") (emphasis added).

[39] *Hilton v. Guyot*, 159 U.S. 113 (1895).

[40] *Id.* at 162.

[41] *See* De la Mata v. Am. Life Ins. Co., 771 F. Supp. 1375, 1382 (D. Del. 1991) ("Courts and commentators have almost universally rejected or ignored the doctrine that reciprocity should be required as a precondition to the recognition and enforcement of a foreign country's judgment."). *See also* RESTATEMENT (THIRD) FOREIGN RELATIONS LAW § 481

The SPEECH Act: The Federal Response to "Libel Tourism"   43

note 1 ("[T]he great majority of courts in the United States have rejected the requirement of reciprocity ...").

[42] United Kingdom, Foreign Judgments (Reciprocal Enforcement) Act 1933, Chap. 13 23_and_24_Geo_5, pt. 1, § 1.

[43] *Hilton*, 159 U.S. at 163-64.

[44] *Id.*

[45] *Id.* at 202-03. Reciprocity is sometimes included as an additional requirement. In *Hilton*, the Court ultimately declined to enforce a French judgment, despite the judgment's fulfillment of these other requirements, because French courts would not enforce a similar judgment rendered by a U.S. court. *Id.* at 227-228.

[46] The *Hilton* decision established the comity principle for federal courts applying federal common law. Later, in *Erie Railroad Co. v. Tomkins*, 304 U.S. 64 (1938), the Supreme Court held that there is no federal common law. Thus, although the *Hilton* decision no longer binds any U.S. court, its articulation has been incorporated into state common law by multiple states' courts.

[47] *See* Gary B. Born & Peter B. Rutledge, *International Civil Litigation in United States Courts* 1013 (2007).

[48] The uniform laws are model statutes drafted by legal experts under the auspices of the National Conference of Commissioners of Uniform State Laws. States can voluntarily adopt a uniform act as state law.

[49] Nat'l Conf. of Comm. of Uniform State Laws, *Unif. Foreign Money Judgments Recognition Act* (approved in 1962), *http://www.law.upenn.edu/bll/archives/ulc/fnact99/1920_69/ufmjr* a62.pdf; Nat'l Conf. of Comm. of Uniform State Laws, *Unif. Foreign-Country Money Judgments Recognition Act* (approved in 2005), http://www.law.upenn.edu/bll/ archives/ulc/ufmjra/2005final.pdf. These uniform acts were drafted by the National Conference of Commissioners on Uniform State Laws, a group that drafts uniform state laws in a range of areas. The prefatory note to the 1962 model explained that the model statute "states rules that [had] long been applied by the majority of courts in this country." 1962 Unif. Act at 1.

[50] 1962 Unif. Act at §§ 2, 3; 2005 Unif. Act at §§ 3, 4.

[51] *Laker Airways v. Sabena, Belgian World Airlines*, 731 F.2d 909, 937 (D.C. Cir. 1984). *See also* Born & Rutledge, *International Civil Litigation in United States Courts* at 1061-62.

[52] 1962 Unif. Act at § 4(3).

[53] 2005 Unif. Act at § 4(c)(3).

[54] *Id.*

[55] *See id.* at § 4, cmt. 8.

[56] *See, e.g., Telnikoff v. Matusevitch*, 702 A.2d 230, 251 (Md. 1997) (refusing to recognize an English libel judgment because it conflicted with Maryland's public policy concerning freedom of the press and defamation actions); *Bachchan v. India Abroad Pubs., Inc.*, 585 N.Y.S.2d 661 (Sup. Ct. N.Y. Cty. 1992) (refusing to recognize a British libel judgment under the public policy exception in New York's foreign judgment recognition statute on ground that British libel law did not accord the protection to free speech and press embodied in U.S. and state constitutions); *Yahoo!, Inc. v. La Ligue Contre le Racisme et L'Anti-semitisme*, 169 F. Supp.2d 1181 (N.D.Cal. 2001) (refusing to enforce an order of a French court, which required an Internet service provider (ISP) to block French citizens' access to Nazi material displayed or offered for sale on the ISP's U.S. site on ground that order's content and viewpoint-based regulation "clearly" would be inconsistent with First Amendment), *rev'd and remanded with instructions to dismiss*, 433 F.3d 1199 (9th Cir. 2006), *cert. denied*, 126 S.Ct. 2332 (2006).

[57] 2008 N.Y. Laws 66.

[58] N.Y. CPLR § 5304(b)(8).

[59] 735 ILCS 5/12-621(b)(7); Fla. Stat. § 55.605(2)(h). A very similar provision in California provides that a court in that state "is not required to recognize" foreign defamation

44 Emily C. Barbour

judgments "unless the court determines that the defamation law applied by the foreign court provided at least as much protection for freedom of speech and the press as provided by both the United States and California Constitutions." Cal. Civ. Pro. Code § 1716(c)(9).

[60] All of the states' foreign judgment recognition statutes—reflecting provisions in the uniform acts—had already provided that foreign judgments need not be recognized if "the cause of action on which the judgment is based is repugnant to the public policy" of the state. 735 ILCS 5/12-621(b)(3); N.Y. CPLR § 5304(b)(4); Cal. Civ. Pro. Code § 1716(c)(3); Fla. Stat. § 555.605(2)(c).

[61] N.Y. CPLR § 302(d). New York's statute authorizes personal jurisdiction over "any person who obtains a judgment in a defamation proceeding outside the United States" against (1) a New York resident, (2) a person with assets in New York, or (3) a person who may have to take actions in New York to comply with the judgment.

[62] Fla. Stat. § 55.6055. The Florida statute tracks New York's but adds a fourth category of persons or entities who are "amenable to jurisdiction" in Florida.

[63] Cal. Civ. Pro. Code § 1717(c). The California statute includes the same four categories but makes it a condition that the foreign judgment was obtained against a California resident or a person or entity amenable to jurisdiction there and requires both (1) that the publication at issue was published in California; and (2) the person against whom the judgment might be enforced either has assets in California that may be sought in an enforcement action or may otherwise "have to take actions in California to comply with the foreign-country defamation judgment."

[64] A court's assertion of personal jurisdiction over a particular defendant must be both constitutional and statutorily authorized. Thus, even if a state or federal statute expressly authorizes jurisdiction over litigants from foreign libel suits, a court might lack jurisdiction under the due process clauses of the Fifth or Fourteenth Amendments to the U.S. Constitution. In cases brought in state courts or against U.S. defendants, the personal jurisdiction analysis implicates the Fourteenth Amendment Due Process Clause. In these cases, the Supreme Court has held that personal jurisdiction is constitutional if defendants have had "minimum contacts" in the judicial forum, such that the assertion of jurisdiction "does not offend traditional notions of fair play and substantial justice." *Int'l Shoe Co. v. Washington*, 326 U.S. 310, 316 (1945) (internal quotations omitted). In some cases, the defendant must have "purposefully availed" himself of the privilege of carrying out activities in the forum, meaning that a defendant's activities in the forum were such that the defendant should have "reasonably anticipated," rather than merely been able to foresee, the possibility of being haled into court there. *World-Wide Volkswagen Corp. v. Woodson*, 444 U.S. 286, 297 (1980). The federal appellate case most relevant to the exercise of personal jurisdiction in suits against plaintiffs in foreign libel suits is *Yahoo! Inc. v. La Ligue Contre Le Racisme Et L'Antisemitisme*, 433 F.3d 1199 (9th Cir. 2006) (per curiam). In *Yahoo!*, an *en banc* panel of the U.S. Court of Appeals for the Ninth Circuit determined that courts in California had personal jurisdiction over two French organizations whose only U.S. contacts included actions connected with their libel suit against Yahoo! in France. *Id.* at 1205.

[65] N.Y. CPLR § 302(d).

[66] Ehrenfeld v. Mahfouz, No. 04 Civ. 8641, 2006 U.S. Dist. LEXIS 23423, at *2 (S.D. N.Y April 25, 2006). Although he successfully fought Ehrenfeld's suit for declaratory judgment, as of June 20, 2009, bin Mahfouz had not sought to have his award for damages enforced in the state of New York. *See* Robert Sharp, *Anti-Free Speech? UK Courts Can Help*, THE GUARDIAN, June 20, 2009, *as corrected on* June 29, 2009, *available at* http://www.guardian.co.uk/ commentisfree/libertycentral/2009/jun/20/libel-tourism-uk-free-speech ("The article below was amended to delete an incorrect statement that Sheikh Bin Mahfouz had sought to have his award for damages enforced in the state of New York. This has been changed."). He died on August 23, 2009. Douglas Martin, *Khalid bin Mahfouz,*

The SPEECH Act: The Federal Response to "Libel Tourism" 45

Saudi Banker, Dies at 60, N.Y. TIMES, Aug. 27, 2009, *available at http://www.n ytimes.com/2009/08/28/world/middleeast/28mahfouz.html.*

[67] *E.g.*, Free Speech Protection Act of 2009, S. 449 and H.R. 1304, 111th Cong. 1st Sess.; Securing the Protection of our Enduring and Established Constitutional Heritage Act (SPEECH Act), S. 3518 and H.R. 2764, 111th Cong., 1st Sess.

[68] P.L. 111-223 *codified at* 28 U.S.C. §§ 4101-4105.

[69] S. 449, § 3(a), (b); H.R. 1304, § 3(a), (b).

[70] *See* H.Rept. 111-154, at 6 (2009) (characterizing the constitutional effects of this approach). *See also World-Wide Volkswagen Corp. v. Woodson*, 444 U.S. 286, 297 (1980); *Int'l Shoe Co. v. Washington*, 326 U.S. 310, 316 (1945); *supra* note 64 and accompanying discussion.

[71] H.Rept. 111-154, at 6 (2009). *But see id.* at 10 (stating the additional views of Senator Jon Kyl that "Congress needs to pass broader measures that permit U.S. citizens accused of libel in foreign courts to force their accusers to pay for legal fees incurred abroad and, in certain cases, additional damages...."). The Committee also wrote that principles of international comity suggested that these counter-suits might represent too great an intrusion into the legal systems of other countries. *Id.*

[72] 28 U.S.C. § 4102.

[73] *See, e.g., Are Foreign Libel Lawsuits Chilling Americans' First Amendment Rights?: Hearing Before the S. Comm. on the Judiciary*, 111th Cong. (Feb. 23, 2010) (written testimony of Kurt Wimmer, Partner, Covington & Burling), http://judiciary.senate.gov/hearings/testim ony.cfm?id=4414&wit_id=9121 (asserting that because "the very act of rendering a foreign judgment has immediate and damaging effects on [a] publisher or author," a lack of enforcement is insufficient to prevent a chilling effect). *See also* S.Rept. 111-224, at 10 (2010) (stating the additional views of Senator Jon Kyl that "Congress needs to pass broader measures that permit U.S. citizens accused of libel in foreign courts to force their accusers to pay for legal fees incurred abroad and, in certain cases, additional damages ... We support this bill as a good first step toward addressing an important problem, but there is more that can, and should, be done.").

[74] Some commentators have noted that, in applying section 230 of the Communications Act of 1934 to foreign judgments, the SPEECH Act only extends protection to *providers* of interactive computer services even though section 230 protects providers and *users* of interactive computer services. *E.g.*, Eric Goldman, *New Anti-Libel Tourism Act (HR 2765) Extends 47 USC 230 to Foreign Judgments*, TECH. & MARKETING L. BLOG (Aug. 11, 2010, 9:20 AM), http://blog.ericgoldman.org.

[75] S.Rept. 111-224, at 7 (2010). *See* 28 U.S.C. § 4101(2).

[76] U.S. CONST. art. VI, cl. 2. *See Gregory v. Ashcroft*, 501 U.S. 452, 460 (1991).

[77] U.S. CONST. art. VI, cl. 2.

[78] *See Spreitsma v. Mercury Marine*, 537 U.S. 51, 64-65 (2002) (quoting *Freightliner Corp. v. Myrick*, 514 U.S. 280, 287 (1995)); *Jones v. Rath Packing Co.*, 430 U.S. 519, 525 (1977).

[79] *Spreitsma*, 537 U.S. at 64-65 (quoting *Freightliner Corp. v. Myrick*, 514 U.S. 280, 287 (1995));

[80] *See Geier v. Honda Motor Co.*, 529 U.S. 861, 873 (2000) ("The Court has not previously driven a legal wedge—only a terminological one—between 'conflicts' that prevent or frustrate the accomplishment of a federal objective and 'conflicts' that make it 'impossible' for private parties to comply with both state and federal law ... it has assumed that Congress would not want either kind of conflict.").

[81] *See* David A. Dana, *Democratizing the Law of Federal Preemption*, 102 NW. U. L. REV. 507, 510 (2008). *E.g., Metro. Life Ins. Co. v. Massachusetts*, 471 U.S. 724, 747 (1985) (stating that congressional intent is the "ultimate touchstone" of preemption analysis).

[82] *See* Dana, *supra* note 81, at 509. *See, e.g., Cipollone v. Liggett Grp.*, 505 U.S. 504, 518-520 (1992) (indicating that the express language of the statute and its legislative history would support a finding of preemption of state statutes).

[83] 28 U.S.C. § 4101(2) ("The term 'domestic court' means a [f]ederal court or a court of any [s]tate."); 28 U.S.C. § 4102 ("Notwithstanding any other provision of [f]ederal or [s]tate

law, a domestic court shall not recognize or enforce a foreign judgment for defamation unless ..." certain criteria are met.). *See Gregory*, 501 U.S. at 466-67 (stating that it can be sufficiently plain to anyone reading a federal law that it preempts conflicting state law even in the absence of explicit language).

[84] S.Rept. 111-224, at 7 (2010); H.Rept. 111-154, at 9 (2009).

[85] *See* Mary J. Davis, *Unmasking the Presumption in Favor of Preemption*, 53 S. C. L. REV. 967, 1016 (2002) ("The perceived need for uniformity of standards is, and has always been, a critical factor to the Court in evaluating whether a state law stands as an obstacle to the accomplishment of federal objectives."). *E.g.*, Geier, 529 U.S. at 871-71 (identifying that the need for uniformity in safety standards was a concern behind the legislation and favored preemption of state safety standards); Rice v. Santa Fe Elevator Corp., 331 U.S. 218, 234-35 (1947) (indicating that the need for national harmonization of warehouse regulations supported preemption).

[86] Viet D. Dinh, *Reassessing the Law of Preemption*, 88 GEO. L. J. 2085, 2086 (2000). *See* Gregory, 501 U.S. at 460-61.

[87] *See* U.S. CONST. art. I, § 8 (enumerating Congress's legislative powers). *See also* Dinh, *supra* note 86, at 2091 ("Preemption is not a substantive power of Congress, but rather a method of regulation in furtherance of some other substantive congressional authority. The power to preempt, therefore, is necessarily pendant on some enumerated power to regulate under Article I, Section 8.").

[88] Dinh, *supra* note 86, at 2086. *E.g.*, Buckman Co. v. Plaintiffs' Legal Comm., 531 U.S. 341, 347 (2001) (suggesting that only federal regulation in a "field the states have traditionally occupied" will "warrant a presumption against finding federal preemption of a state law cause of action."); Medtronic, Inc. v. Lohr, 518 U.S. 470, 485 (1996) ("[B]ecause the [s]tates are independent sovereigns in our federal system, we have long presumed that Congress does not cavalierly pre-empt state-law causes of action."). *But see* Davis, *supra* note 85, at 968-971 (arguing that Supreme Court's "preemption analysis has, in effect, created a presumption *in favor* of preemption, contrary to the Court' oft-quoted dicta that there is a presumption *against* preemption ...").

[89] Dana, *supra* note 81, at 515.

[90] However, Congress has imposed restrictions on state courts in the past. *See, e.g.*, Foreign Assistance Act of 1961, Pub. L. 87-195, § 620(e)(2), *as amended and codified at* 22 U.S.C. § 2370(e)(2) (providing that, unless the President intervened or certain other circumstances existed, "no court in the United States shall decline on the ground of the federal act of state doctrine to make a determination on the merits giving effect to the principle of international law in a case in which the claim of title or other rights to property is asserted by any party ..."); Cuban Liberty and Democratic Solidarity (LIBERTAD) Act of 1996, P.L. 104-114, § 302(a)(6) *codified at* 22 U.S.C. § 6082(a)(6) (providing that "[n]o court of the United States shall decline, based upon the act of state doctrine, to make a determination on the merits in an action brought under" § 302(a)(1) of the act, establishing a civil remedy against persons trafficking in property confiscated by Cuba claimed by U.S. nationals).

[91] LOUIS HENKIN, FOREIGN AFFAIRS AND THE UNITED STATES CONSTITUTION 70 (2d ed. 1996). *See* U.S. CONST. art. I, § 8, cl. 1, 3, 10, 11, 15, 18. *See also* Zschernig v. Miller, 389 U.S. 429, 432 (1968) (stating that the field of foreign affairs is entrusted by the Constitution to the President and to the Congress).

[92] *See* William S. Dodge, *Antitrust and the Draft Hague Judgments Convention*, 32 LAW & POL'Y INT'L BUS 363, 363 (2001) ("Other countries have long resisted the extraterritorial application of U.S. antitrust law. Several have passed blocking statutes to hinder the discovery of evidence that might be useful in such cases. The United Kingdom has provided, by legislation, that U.S. antitrust judgments are not enforceable in British courts, and both Australia and Canada have given their Attorneys General authority to declare such judgments unenforceable or to reduce the amounts that will be enforced.").

[93] For example, in the context of antitrust law, the United States has negotiated bilateral agreements with countries who have enacted blocking statutes and thereby obtained the foreign country's assurance that its blocking statute will not be triggered solely by U.S. efforts to use legal processes to procure evidence for an antitrust case in that country. *E.g.*, Agreement Relating to Cooperation on Antitrust Matters, Art. 5, U.S.-Aus., June 29, 1982, 34 UST 388. *See also* Roger P. Alford, *The Extraterritorial Application of Antitrust Laws: The United States and European Community Approaches*, 33 VA. J. INT'L L. 1, 47 n. 225 (1992) (identifying several bilateral consultation agreements between the United States and foreign countries); Harold G. Maier, *Interest Balancing and Extraterritorial Jurisdiction*, 31 AM. J. COMP. L. 578, 587 (1983) (describing the United States-Australian antitrust agreement's effect on Australia's blocking statute). The United States also has a history of opposing international initiatives to harmonize antitrust law. Spencer Weber Waller, *National Laws and International Markets: Strategies of Cooperation and Harmonization in the Enforcement of Competition Law*, 18 CARDOZO L. REV. 1111, 1118 (1996).

In: Libel Tourism and Foreign Libel Lawsuits ISBN: 978-1-61209-148-8
Editor: Amy J. Brower © 2011 Nova Science Publishers, Inc.

Chapter 3

TESTIMONY OF DR. RACHEL EHRENFELD, DIRECTOR OF THE AMERICAN CENTER FOR DEMOCRACY, BEFORE THE SUBCOMMITTEE ON COMMERCIAL AND ADMINISTRATIVE LAW, HEARING ON "LIBEL TOURISM"

SUMMARY

Thank you, Mr. Chairman and members of the Committee, for holding this hearing, which touches me personally. My special thanks to Chairman Cohen for inviting me. In addition to my oral testimony, I submit my written statement for the record.

We are confronted by libel tourism -- a pernicious and growing phenomenon, especially after the 9/11 attacks on America -- whereby wealthy and corrupt terror financiers exploit plaintiff-friendly foreign libel laws and expansive Internet jurisdiction to silence American authors and publishers. Foreign libel laws have become a potent weapon used by the forces of tyranny who seek to undermine our freedom. The Free Speech Protection Act can stop this.

In *New York Times v. Sullivan*, the Supreme Court struck a critical balance between libel actions and a free press guaranteed by the First Amendment. The high court raised the bar for libel plaintiffs to insure our "profound national commitment to the principle that debate on public issues should be uninhibited, robust, and wide-open." Based on that principle, the court declared: "libel can claim no talismanic immunity from constitutional limitations."

Outside the United States, there are no such "constitutional limitations." The House of Lords explicitly rejected the *Sullivan* standard. So did the Canadian Supreme Court. Although all forty-one-member states of the Council of Europe submit to the European Court of Human Rights, Article 10 of its charter also rejects the *Sullivan* standard.

In many countries, journalists can be jailed for criminal libel; truth is often not a defense; high office holders enjoy extra protection against criticism; publications can be confiscated; newspapers and broadcast stations can be shuttered; and writers can be forced to publish adverse court orders, and repudiate as false what they know to be true.

Congress must protect American writers and publishers to guarantee the "uninhibited, robust and wide-open" debate the First Amendment was designed to protect. Scholars like me seek Congress's help to stop libel tourism from limiting our ability to write freely about important matters of public policy vital to our national security.

I can attest that libel tourism is costly, financially and emotionally. I do not command an army - or control an industry - or have vast wealth - or hold political office. In other words, I do not possess any traditional sources of power in society. Instead, I write. I am a scholar dedicated to expose the enemies of freedom and Western democracy. I expend great time and effort tracking down information across the globe. My books and articles are based in large part on evidence presented to Congress, parliaments and courts. Like most responsible scholars, I publish only material that can be verified. My credibility and livelihood depend on it.

In 1992, I published *Narcoterrorism: How Governments Around the World Have Used the Drug Trade to Finance and Further Terrorist Activities,* and first called attention to the intimate relationship between drug trafficking and terrorism.

Terrorism is not cheap. To the contrary, it is a capital-intensive activity. It requires lots of cash for training, weapons, vehicles, salaries, cell phones, airline travel, food and lodging; etc. I showed how the drug trade, not just oil profits, fuels terrorist organizations. While policy makers were romanticizing the Palestine Liberation Organization as a group of so-called "freedom fighters," I showed how the PLO filled its coffers with billions of dollars from heroin, hashish, airplane highjacking, extortion and illegal arms sales. Until my book, neither the American government nor international agencies for drug control publicly linked narcotics and terrorism.

Testimony of Dr. Rachel Ehrenfeld, Director of the American Center... 51

When asked why he robbed banks, Willy Sutton famously replied: "Because that's where the money is." I followed his lead and followed the money. This led to my second book, *Evil Money: The Inside Story of Money Laundering and Corruption in Government, Banks and Business,* in which I connected the dots between drug profits, money laundering, political corruption, Islamic banking and how illicit funds are used to undermine democracies.

The Committee undoubtedly remembers BCCI, the Bank of Credit and Commerce International, the cash till for Hezbollah, the PLO, HAMAS, Abu Nidal and other terrorist organizations. BCCI's chief operating officer was Saudi billionaire, Khalid bin Mahfouz, banker to the Saudi royal family and at that time, owner of the National Commercial Bank of Saudi Arabia. In 1992, Mahfouz paid $225 million to settle criminal charges against him in New York arising from his control of BCCI.

In 2003, I published my third book, *Funding Evil, How Terrorism is Financed and How to Stop It.* In that book, I showed the true face of terrorism. It is not the stereotype of underprivileged Islamic youth yearning to be religious martyrs, but instead, an international network of corrupt dictators, drug kingpins, and villains like Mahfouz who transferred some $74 million to at least two front charities for terrorism: the International Islamic Relief Organization and his Muwafaq or "blessed relief" Foundation, which then gave the funds directly to al Qaeda, Hamas and other radical Muslim organizations.

In response, Mahfouz sued me for libel. What happened to me did not occur in a dark backwater of totalitarian repression like Syria, Saudi Arabia, or North Korea, but in England. Mahfouz does not live there. I do not live there. My book was not published or marketed there. Nonetheless, the English court accepted jurisdiction because twenty-three copies of *Funding Evil* arrived in England via Internet purchases.

English law does not distinguish between private persons and public figures. Allegedly, offensive statements are presumed defamatory and the libel defendant bears the burden to prove they are true. Official documents from non-English sources are typically inadmissible in court, and Arab dictatorships refuse to help Western writers and publishers prove allegations about terrorism.

Protection of opinion is limited and multiple suits are allowed for a single act of publication. Libel defendants have limited pre-trial discovery and no right to depose plaintiffs under oath, as in American courts. Thus, libel plaintiffs usually win, verdicts are substantial, and defendants must pay the plaintiff's legal fees. It is no wonder then, the Times of London called London the "libel capital of the Western world."

Mahfouz's threats conveyed by E-mails, faxes, and legal papers were unsettling, and on one occasion, I was warned to do as he demanded if I "knew what was good for me" because he has friends in high places who wield great influence in the U.S.

I refused to recognize the English court's jurisdiction because I should not have to defend myself abroad. The British court granted Mahfouz a default judgment and awarded him hundreds of thousands of dollars; required me to prevent copies of *Funding Evil* from reaching Britain; and ordered me to publish retractions drafted by his solicitors.

Libel tourism by Mahfouz and others like him made me realize something more was at stake than my book and the particulars involving him. In response, I sued Mahfouz in New York to declare his English judgment violated my rights under the First Amendment. That litigation led the New York Legislature last May to enact New York's version of the Free Speech Protection Act. Illinois followed suit last August.

Until the new statute protected me -- dubbed by the media as "Rachel's Law" -- Mahfouz's English judgment hung over my head like a sword of Damocles and kept me up at night.

The United States has a tradition of almost automatic enforcement of foreign judgments under the doctrine of comity enshrined in the Uniform Foreign Money-Judgments Recognition Act adopted by a majority of states. Although writers can assert a First Amendment defense to enforcement actions, few have the economic resources to do so.

Hence, libel tourism forces them to engage in self-censorship. Mahfouz's libel tourism in London led American publishers with assets abroad to cancel several books under contract or consideration. Those who once willingly courted my work now refuse to publish me. In nearly forty cases, Mahfouz obtained settlements against his victims, all with forced apologies, by the mere threat of libel litigation. His boasts about this on his website to effectively silence and intimidate his critics in the media and academia.

Case law speaks of the "chilling effect" on free speech threatened by unrestrained libel actions. My case demonstrates the chilling effect is no mere abstraction. I cannot travel to the U.K., lest I be arrested to enforce Mahfouz's extant judgment, and I run the same risk in Europe, due to the European Community's reciprocal enforcement of member states' judgments. Similar laws apply in most Commonwealth states, too.

I close with the immortal words of Justice Brandeis in *Whitney v. California*:

> Those who won our independence believed that the final end of the state was to make men free to develop their facilities, and that in its government the deliberative forces should prevail over the arbitrary .... They believed that freedom to think as you will and to speak as you think are means indispensable to the discovery and spread of political truth .... Believing in the power of reason as applied through public discussion, they eschewed silence coerced by law – the argument of force in its worst form. Recognizing the occasional tyrannies of governing majorities, they amended the Constitution so that free speech and assembly should be guaranteed.

A free press is vital not only to our lifestyles, but also, to our national security to protect writers like me who expose those who do us evil. New York and Illinois have enacted laws to protect their citizens from the scourge of libel tourism which threatens press freedom and scholars, writers and publishers everywhere. The federal Free Speech Protection Act insures all American citizens will enjoy such protection. Congress should pass it without delay.

Dr. Rachel Ehrenfeld
Brief bio:

Dr. Rachel Ehrenfeld is the Director of the New York-based American Center for Democracy and the Center for the Study of Corruption & the Rule of Law. She is the author of *Funding Evil: How Terrorism is Financed - and How to Stop It* (BonusBooks, 2003, 2005); *Evil Money* (HarperCollins, 1992, SPI, 1994) and *Narco-Terrorism* (Basic Books, 1990, 1992).

Dr. Ehrenfeld is an expert on the shadowy movement of funds through international banking, governments and businesses to fund terrorism. She has a unique understanding of the challenges of international terrorism to democracy and freedom, and how money laundering and political corruption facilitates terror financing and economic warfare.

An American citizen fluent in several languages, Ehrenfeld has testified before Congressional Committees, as well as the European and Canadian Parliaments, provided evidence to the British Parliament, and has been a consultant to foreign governments as well as U.S. government agencies such as the Departments of State and Defense, Treasury, Justice, the CIA, and Homeland Security. She is also a Member of the Board of Directors of the Committee on the Present Danger.

She has been a visiting scholar at the Columbia University Institute of War and Peace Studies, a research scholar at the New York University School of Law, and a fellow at Johns Hopkins School of Advanced International Studies, Fletcher School of Law and Diplomacy and Jesus College at Cambridge University. She has a PhD in Criminology from the Hebrew University School of Law.

Her articles have appeared in numerous publications such as The New York Times, Forbes, Los Angeles Times, The Jerusalem Post, The Wall Street Journal and the Huffington Post, and she is a frequent guest on domestic and international TV and radio.

In: Libel Tourism and Foreign Libel Lawsuits ISBN: 978-1-61209-148-8
Editor: Amy J. Brower © 2011 Nova Science Publishers, Inc.

Chapter 4

TESTIMONY OF BRUCE D. BROWN, BAKER & HOSTETLER LLP, BEFORE THE SUBCOMMITTEE ON COMMERCIAL AND ADMINISTRATIVE LAW, HEARING ON "LIBEL TOURISM"

Mr. Chairman and Members of the Subcommittee:

I am Bruce D. Brown, a partner at Baker & Hostetler LLP in Washington, D.C. We represent clients ranging from large media companies to book and magazine publishers to journalism advocacy organizations such as the Society of Professional Journalists. I worked for David Broder at the Washington Post for two years prior to law school, received my J.D. from Yale in 1995, and then worked as a reporter at Legal Times covering the federal courts before joining my law firm. I am the co-chair of the legislative affairs committee of the Media Law Resource Center in New York and am an adjunct faculty member in Georgetown University's master's program in Professional Studies in Journalism.

I am honored to appear before the subcommittee today to discuss the phenomenon known as libel tourism and to assist the subcommittee in any way I can to illustrate the urgency in finding a legislative remedy for a problem that is distorting and diminishing First Amendment protections in the U.S. In this written testimony, I provide the subcommittee with evidence of recent cases in which the differences between U.S. and U.K. libel law have created an incentive for foreign plaintiffs to sue American publishers in England even when their connection to the U.K. is non-existent or tenuous at best. This trend has enabled overseas litigants to intimidate U.S. authors with the fear of large verdicts in Britain, thus reducing the amount of information the public receives here at home because of the resulting chilling effect.

While there is some reason to believe that this abuse of the English courts is finally starting to attract the attention of reform-minded U.K. lawmakers, I support efforts by this subcommittee to press ahead with legislation to curb this growing threat and protect First Amendment interests. Countering the impact of libel tourism is not about second-guessing the British people for coming to a different balance between reputation interests and freedom of speech than we have, it is about making sure that foreign jurisdictions do not dictate to us how we should strike this balance for ourselves.

"From Plassey to Pakistan" – and on to London

To understand the menace of libel tourism, the subcommittee need go no further than several miles up Connecticut Avenue to Bethesda, Maryland, where author Humayun Mirza lives. Mr. Mirza, who spent more than 30 years working in finance at the World Bank, turned to writing only after his retirement. He devoted years to composing a biography of his father, Iskander Mirza, the first President of Pakistan. "From Plassey to Pakistan: The Family History of Iskander Mirza," was published by Lanham, Maryland-based University Press of America in November 1999.

This scholarly work took readers back through more than 300 years of Indian and Pakistani history from the perspective of the Nawab Nazims who ruled Bengal, Bihar and Orissa. It explored the events leading to the British rule of India, India's independence, and Pakistan's secession from India. From there, Mr. Mirza documented his father's rise to power as a secular leader as well as the military *coup d'état* that led to his father's exile. Through the book's more than 400 pages, Mr. Mirza wove together the historical origins of this volatile region and the fortunes of generations of his family who bore witness to it all.

But shortly after publication, University Press received a letter from the U.K. attorneys of Begum Nahid Mirza, the second wife of Mr. Mirza's father, complaining of libel and threatening to sue in the U.K. Mr. Mirza had written about the Begum Mirza only in connection with her relationship with his father, and each statement was founded on firsthand observations, decades of

Testimony of Bruce D. Brown, Baker & Hostetler LLP, before... 57

conversations with family members and Pakistani leaders, and official documents from the U.S. Department of State. Stated more succinctly, the book was a well-researched work of scholarship and historical interpretation that would unquestionably have been protected under U.S. law. "From Plassey to Pakistan" was hardly distributed in the U.K., but the Begum Mirza, who had a residence in the U.K., had lined up one of London's leading law firms – a firm that has since played a prominent role in the libel tourism industry – to attempt to scare Mr. Mirza into withdrawing his book. She was able to do this because of the many advantages she would enjoy as a libel plaintiff in the U.K. courts.

For example, under U.S. law, a libel plaintiff has the burden of showing that the statements at issue were false – a requirement that the Begum Mirza could never have satisfied. In the U.K., however, the defendant has the burden of proving the truth of the statements – a much more difficult (and costly) proposition for any author or publisher. Moreover, English courts do not require, as American courts have since *New York Times Co. v. Sullivan*, 376 U.S. 254 (1964), that a plaintiff must prove that allegedly defamatory statements about public officials or public figures were published with "actual malice," or clear and convincing evidence that the author was aware that the statements were false or made them with reckless disregard for the truth. (Only recently has England recognized a qualified privilege for defendants who act "responsibly" but this privilege is no substitute for *New York Times* protections or the shield of the fair report privilege as it has evolved in U.S. courts.[1]) Under American law, the Begum Mirza, whose status as the wife of a former head of state makes her a public figure, would have had no evidence with which to prove that the author published with actual malice. In fact, Mr. Mirza made several unsuccessful attempts to contact her for her side of the story, evidence which would have tended to protect him in a U.S. court because it was a sign of his effort to find and publish the truth. A chart of the constitutional protections in U.S. libel law, organized by the status of the plaintiff, is attached as Exhibit A.

These protections at the trial level are all supported by the unique constitutional commitment by appellate courts in the U.S. to conduct "independent appellate review" in libel cases to ensure that any judgment awarded to a plaintiff "does not constitute a forbidden intrusion on the field of free expression."[2] This probing standard, enunciated in *Bose Corp. v. Consumers Union of U.S.*, 466 U.S. 485 (1984), requires judges to deviate from the typical standard of appellate review of jury verdicts by examining the entire record and substituting their own judgment for that of the jury on

58 Bruce D. Brown

matters relating to the weighing of evidence and the drawing of interferences. As a result, as the Media Law Resource Center has been diligently documenting for years, more than 70 percent of libel verdicts are overturned on appeal in the U.S.[3] Appellate tribunals in the U.K. have no analogue to the *Bose* rule.

As a result of the deep chasm between American and British libel law, and the enormous burden of trying to prove the truth of matters that took place nearly half a century earlier in Pakistan, Mr. Mirza and his publisher faced the very real probability that they could be held liable in Britain for something they had every right to publish in the U.S., where the vast majority of their readers could be found. After more than a year of negotiation with the Begum Mirza, they reached a settlement and the first edition of the book was destroyed. The threat of significant damages, in addition to attorney's fees to the plaintiff if she prevailed, was simply too much to risk.

THE EVOLUTION OF LIBEL TOURISM

Until the mid-1990s, the difference in U.S. and U.K. libel law was a subject largely confided to academic journals and law school classrooms. Then, in 1996, controversial English historian David Irving sued Emory University Professor Deborah Lipstadt in London for defamation after she properly and accurately called him a "Holocaust denier."[4] The Irving-Lipstadt case became international news, bringing to the forefront the salient divide between U.S. and U.K. defamation standards. Professor Lipstadt assumed that the suit would be a minor inconvenience, but she soon learned exactly why being sued in England is so damaging to an American author.[5] It was only after five-year ordeal that culminated in a 10-day trial and cost upwards of $3 million that she escaped liability.[6]

For me, watching the Lipstadt case unfold and then handling the Mirza matter shortly thereafter, it was apparent that with the arrival of the Internet, while the world was shrinking, the disparity between U.S. and U.K. libel was not – and that this tension was only going to grow. I wrote a piece on the subject for the Washington Post, which the newspaper called, "Write Here. Libel There. So Beware."[7] The headline writers knew what they were talking about.

On the heels of Professor Lipstadt's trial came the case that opened a new phase in the transatlantic free speech rift – lawsuits brought in England by

Testimony of Bruce D. Brown, Baker & Hostetler LLP, before... 59

plaintiffs who are *not* U.K. residents but who sue in that jurisdiction to exploit its plaintiff-friendly libel laws. The practice earned a neat nickname – "libel tourism." In 1997, Russian tycoon Boris Berezovsky filed suit against Forbes magazine in London over an article from the December 1996 issue of the magazine titled "Godfather of the Kremlin?"[8] The piece, written by Russian-American journalist Paul Klebnikov, portrayed Berezovsky as a man who, as Forbes pointed out in a related editorial, was followed by "a trail of corpses, uncollectible debts and competitors terrified for their lives."[9] Forbes argued that it made no sense to litigate a case involving a Russian plaintiff and a New York magazine in England, where a tiny fraction of the publication's readers were located and which was not a focal point of the reporting. But the English courts would not loosen their grips on the suit, and Forbes eventually retracted the claims and settled the case rather than face trial.[10] Klebnikov was murdered on a Moscow street in 2004.[11]

Fueled by the boom in Internet publishing that wiped out traditional, "real-world" jurisdictional lines across the globe, billionaires and politicians soon flocked – virtually, at least – to England to settle their scores where they knew the deck was stacked in their favor. Libel tourism's most frequent flier is the Saudi businessman Khalid bin Mahfouz, who notoriously sued American author Rachel Ehrenfeld for documenting evidence of his financial ties to terrorism in her book "Funding Evil: How Terrorism is Financed – and How to Stop It." Ms. Ehrenfeld may have been bin Mahfouz's most famous target, but she is not his only victim. In fact, Mr. bin Mahfouz has proudly posted a website identifying the many authors and publishers who have been intimidated by his courtroom tactics and have recanted or settled U.K. lawsuits that he has filed.[12] The chilling effect of Mr. bin Mahfouz's litigation campaign is clear.

Americans are not the only ones harmed by libel tourism. In the past few years alone,

- Ekstra Baladet, a tabloid newspaper in Denmark, was sued in the U.K. by Kaupthing, an investment bank in Iceland, over articles that were critical about the bank's advice to its wealthy clients about tax shelters. The bank and the newspaper are still litigating the dispute in a system, the newspaper notes, in which it is forced to pay five times as much to litigate the case than it would in Denmark.[13]
- A Dubai-based satellite television network, Al Arabiya, was successfully sued in England by a Tunisian businessman who, like Mr. bin Mahfouz, disputed allegations that he had ties to terrorist

60 Bruce D. Brown

groups. The station chose not to defend the charges and the Tunisian businessman was awarded $325,000.[14]

- Rinat Akhmetov, one of the Ukraine's richest men, filed lawsuits against two Ukranian-based news organizations. In one case, the Kyiv Post quickly settled and apologized. In the other, Mr. Akhmetov won a default judgment of $75,000 against Obozrevatel, a Ukranian-based internet news site that publishes articles in Ukranian.[15]

But the stark contrast between American and English libel law makes the effect of libel tourism that much more injurious on publishers and authors based in the U.S.

Moreover, the problem of libel tourism is only amplified by the willingness of English courts to allow plaintiffs with little connection to the U.K. to sue over publications that were in no way "aimed" at the jurisdiction – the test that U.S. courts apply as a matter of due process before subjecting a defendant to personal jurisdiction. This constraint is particularly important in the context of libel actions based on publication over the Internet because online content can be viewed anywhere around the world. *See Young v. New Haven Advocate*, 315 F.3d 256 (4th Cir. 2002). For the U.K. courts, the almost 2,000 copies of Forbes distributed in England (as opposed to the nearly 800,000 sold in the U.S.) were enough to create personal jurisdiction over the magazine in London.[16] In Ms. Ehrenfeld's case, only 23 copies of her book found their way into the hands of British citizens.[17] In the case of the Danish publisher mentioned above, the articles were available as an English translation on a Danish website that received very little traffic in England.[18] And in the case of Al Arabiya, the program in question was available in Britain only by satellite.[19]

As one British lawyer who frequently represents media defendants has noted, British courts, "somewhat sadly, are reluctant to give up jurisdiction," even where the facts giving rise to the allegations have almost no tie to the U.K.[20] English judges are also disinclined to throw out a lawsuit on *forum non conveniens* grounds, the legal doctrine that permits dismissal where personal jurisdiction over the defendant is established but where the practicalities of litigating in that jurisdiction dictate that the case should be heard somewhere else.[21] As a result, libel plaintiffs find England a very hospitable place to sue American authors, and, the laws of supply and demand being what they are, London is home to a plaintiff's media bar with far more resources and far greater numbers than what is found in the U.S. As Ms. Ehrenfeld discovered, U.K. courts are appealing to libel tourists for the additional reason that they will grant injunctions against further publication, a remedy wholly foreign to American jurisprudence with its traditions against prior restraint. For Ms. Ehrenfeld, the injunction against "Funding Evil" was the ultimate insult: she could in theory be held in contempt if a book she never intended for the U.K. audience continued to reach U.K. readers.

A TALE OF TWO PRESSES

In 2007, after Mr. bin Mahfouz sued two American authors who tied him to terrorism, the authors' publisher, Cambridge University Press agreed to pulp all unsold copies of the book, "Alms for Jihad," rather than defend the work.[22] In a letter of apology to Mr. bin Mahfouz, Cambridge University Press wrote that the allegations contained in the book were "entirely and manifestly false" and asked that the Sheikh "accept [its] sincere apologies for the distress and embarrassment [publication] has caused."[23] Cambridge University Press also published an apology on its website noting that it would pay substantial damages and legal costs.[24]

At around the same time, Yale University Press was sued by KinderUSA, a nonprofit group that states that it raises money for Palestinian children and families, and Laila Al-Marayati, the chair of the group's board, over the publication of "Hamas: Politics, Charity, and Terrorism in the Service of Jihad."[25] The suit identified two passages in the book about charitable groups in the U.S. that were linked to terrorist groups and objected to this passage specifically:

> The formation of KinderUSA highlights an increasingly common trend: banned charities continuing to operate by incorporating under new names in response to designation as terrorist entities or in an effort to evade attention. This trend is also seen with groups raising money for al-Qaeda.[26]

KinderUSA also alleged that the statement that it "funds terrorist or illegal organizations" was "false and damaging" and libelous.[27] The plaintiffs sought $500,000 in damages.[28] But in a sudden change of heart shortly after filing its complaint, KinderUSA dismissed the suit.[29]

Why did Yale University Press succeed in defending itself against charges almost identical to those that brought Cambridge University Press to its knees? The two books at issue presented different factual issues, for sure, but Cambridge was sued in England while Yale was sued in California. Yale thus enjoyed the protections of the First Amendment along with the procedural benefits California provides in its anti-SLAPP statute to defendants attacked by frivolous libel suits.[30] Yale took advantage of this law to file a motion to strike the complaint on the grounds that the lawsuit was a blatant attempt to silence legitimate criticism on a matter of public interest. In its motion, Yale called the suit a "classic, meritless challenge to free expression."[31] KinderUSA withdrew the suit before the court could even hear the motion.[32]

My law firm has experience with California's anti-SLAPP statute in a similar case. In 2003, we represented the National Review in a libel suit brought in California by Hussam Ayloush, the executive director of the Southern California chapter of the Council on American-Islamic Relations, against the magazine and its guest columnist, former California Republican Party president Shawn Steel. Mr. Ayloush's complaint concerned Mr. Steel's documentation of anti-Jewish comments made by an Egyptian Islamic leader at a public event co-hosted by Mr. Ayloush and CAIR. The allegations were, as we described them in an anti-SLAPP motion, a "thinly disguised attempt to squelch dissenting views in the rampant public discussion about American-Islamic relations, an issue of utmost importance in the international political milieu." The plaintiff never responded to the motion and the case was dismissed. A libel suit filed by the Islamic Society of Boston against the Boston Herald met a somewhat similar fate in 2007. The action was based on an article that linked the Islamic Society to Abdurahman Alamoudi, a public supporter of terrorist organizations including Hamas and Hezbollah.[33] The Islamic Society's claims collapsed as soon as it began exchanging discovery with the Boston Herald, which we represented, and the Islamic Society quickly dropped its claims.[34]

The dispositions of these last two lawsuits, which share with many of the libel tourism cases a focus on international terrorism and its financing, demonstrate the precise reason why foreign libel plaintiffs avoid U.S. courts and seek capitulation in the friendly confines of the U.K. That the libel tourism cases that have earned the most attention are ones where the actual malice rules would have supplied the U.S. defendant with far greater protections than those available in the U.K. is no accident. While theoretically true that cases brought by private figures involving private matters are not covered by the actual malice rules in the U.S., such disputes are unlikely to land in a British court. Even when U.S. law does not provide constitutional actual malice protections and instead only requires common-law negligence, the American defendant is still better protected in a U.S. court because of other substantive safeguards such as the shifting of the burden to the plaintiff to prove falsity.

THE CHILLING EFFECT OF LIBEL TOURISM

Today's testimony will chronicle several of the well-known examples of libel tourism that have played out in the courts. Each of the panelists has particular experiences to highlight.

But the effects of libel tourism are felt well beyond the known public record. It has created a silent chilling effect that is felt by *any* author or publisher writing about controversial international subjects today. Journalists often find themselves forced to self-censor their speech to ensure not that it meets the standards for First Amendment protection, but instead so that it satisfies the much more stifling strictures of English libel law. While it's nearly impossible to catalogue the smothering pressure of libel tourism on what was *not* published, media lawyers who handle prepublication review know firsthand how libel tourism has changed the legal landscape, particularly in the area of journalism that tackles global terrorism. As Senators Arlen Specter and Joe Lieberman noted in their Wall Street Journal opinion piece on libel tourism last summer, the chilling effect on reporters in the U.S. impacts our national security because its cuts off the flow of information that would otherwise reach the public.[35]

Late last year, I reviewed Robert Spencer's book "Stealth Jihad: How Radical Islam is Subverting America without Guns or Bombs" prior to publication to make sure that it met all appropriate legal standards. Mr. Spencer's book was the sort of well-researched volume with copious notations to material in the public record that would traditionally have hardly been cause for alarm. But I knew that such a title bristled with potential exposure, not because any of the subjects of the book might bring suit in Lahore, but because they might bring suit in London. Even if publishers attempt to prevent wide distribution in England, it is inevitable that copies will end up in the hands of U.K. citizens, as Rachel Ehrenfeld discovered.

Lawyers therefore have no choice but to vet every name mentioned in such a book as well as all supporting documentation. But even with those precautions, which are more than enough to reassure clients that any defamation case brought in the U.S. could be disposed of swiftly, media counsel remain nervous about the risk of exposure in England. We are thus, as part of a new ritual, now routinely informing our clients, whether they be first-time authors, large media companies, participants at a citizen journalism academy sponsored by the Society of Professional Journalists, or the insurance companies that write the libel policies for all of the above, of the calculated risks of publishing in this climate. There are vulnerabilities that previously did not exist.

My colleagues Bruce Sanford, Lee Ellis, Henry Hoberman, and Bob Lystad represented journalist Craig Unger more than a decade ago in a libel suit filed by Robert McFarlane against Esquire magazine over an article on the alleged "October Surprise" at the end of the Carter presidency regarding efforts to negotiate the release of the American hostages in Iran.[36] The U.S. Court of Appeals for the D.C. Circuit affirmed summary judgment in Mr. Unger's favor in 1996 on the grounds that he had no reason to believe anything in his piece was false and thus did not publish with actual malice.[37] Roughly a decade later, Mr. Unger's British publisher cancelled plans to bring his U.S. bestseller "House of Bush, House of Saud: The Secret Relationship Between the World's Two Most Powerful Dynasties" to the U.K. for fear of being sued.[38] Mr. Unger has experienced first-hand the chilling effect of libel tourism.

Book and magazine publishers and metropolitan daily newspapers are increasingly sharing the stage of investigative journalism with nonprofits and other sources of original reporting, such as academic programs at universities. These organizations, too, are subject to the same threat of libel tourism. Students in the master's in journalism program in which I teach at Georgetown University, for example, have been tirelessly tracking down documents, interviewing sources, and gathering information for more than a year about the kidnapping and execution of Wall Street Journal reporter Daniel Pearl while on assignment in Pakistan.[39] The Pearl Project, as it is known, is now a part of the Center for Public Integrity, the well-regarded nonprofit in D.C. that has been publishing independent journalism since 1989. The students and their sponsors expect to release the results of their investigation later this year. Even though their final report will be published here in the U.S., and even though they will be scrupulous in their fact-checking, the project's professors, nonprofit sponsors, and funders face legal uncertainties for their heroic work because of the very nature of what they are seeking to uncover. These students are just learning about the history of the First Amendment and the substantial protections it affords, and they need to be reassured that we are doing everything we can to make sure those protections are not taken away from them by foreign courts.

One major U.S. publisher whom these students would all aspire to write for one day recently paid a substantial sum to avoid a lawsuit in the U.K. even though the reporting was based on government records and even though this publisher has a long and distinguished history in fighting for a free press.

U.K. Reaction to the "International Scandal" of Libel Tourism

The British government is finally starting to come to terms with the problems posed by libel tourists. In December, three influential MPs urged the government to radically reform Britain's libel laws to remedy what the Labour Party's Denis MacShane called the "international scandal" of libel tourism that has turned British courts into a "Soviet-style organ of censorship."[41] He continued:

> It shames Britain and makes a mockery of the idea that Britain is a protector of core democratic freedoms. Libel tourism sounds innocuous, but underneath the banal phrase is a major assault on freedom of information which in today's complex world is more necessary than ever if evil, such as the jihad ideology that led to the Mumbai massacres, is not to flourish, and if those who traffic arms, blood diamonds, drugs and money to support Islamist extremist organisations that hide behind charitable status are not to be exposed.[42]

In response, Justice Minister Bridget Prentice promised to consider the codification of the qualified privilege recognized in the *Reynolds* decision that provides defendants with a public interest defense to charges of libel if they can prove they acted responsibly.[43] She also pledged to give the public a chance to weigh in on British policies regarding defamation and the Internet, to consider whether to abolish criminal libel, and to review the high cost of defending defamation charges in the U.K.[44] *See also* Tim Luckhurst, "For freedom's sake, we must stop libel tourism," THE GUARDIAN, Aug. 15, 2008; Nick Cohen, "A free speech crusade we should all be proud to join," THE EVENING STANDARD, Dec. 11, 2008.

Hearings such as this one highlight the problem and hopefully will encourage the British government to execute reforms so that American reporters who do not purposefully direct their reporting toward or publish their work in the U.K. will not be hauled into English courts to defend journalism that would be fully protected in the U.S.

Solving the Libel Tourism Problem

It is time for Congress to enact legislation to stem the tide of libel tourism. What began as a few isolated incidents has evolved into an industry in London and a sense of vulnerability here in the U.S. about our own constitutional safeguards. After the U.S. Supreme Court constitutionalized the law of libel in *New York Times v. Sullivan*, the American news media hoped for similar reform abroad. That transformation has not materialized over the last 40 years, but the problem with libel tourism is not that U.K. law has refused to evolve along the same path as ours, it is that U.K. law now threatens to undo the free speech protections we have chosen for ourselves at home.

The bills introduced in the 110th Congress were an excellent start to combating libel tourism. In this Congress, this subcommittee faces the challenge of crafting a bill that will not only serve as a powerful deterrent to libel tourists but also that will comport with other constitutional requirements. The starting point for any federal libel tourism statute should be to deny enforcement in domestic courts to overseas defamation judgments that fail under the First Amendment. But to create a robust disincentive, any libel tourism law should additionally provide a cause of action in the federal courts to permit a U.S. publisher subjected to harassing litigation overseas intended to circumvent our free speech protections to countersue and seek money damages against the foreign plaintiff. Without the latter provision, the necessary deterrent will not be achieved. But a federal libel tourism statute must do all of this in a manner consistent with due process. My colleague David B. Rivkin and I have recently expressed reservations about subjecting plaintiffs from foreign lands to the personal jurisdiction of our courts unless they have sufficient minimum contacts with the U.S.[45]

In designing a legislative response to libel tourism, the subcommittee may well find it useful to consider the experience of the states that have implemented anti-SLAPP bills. These state laws provide judges with the tools to make an initial evaluation as to whether an underlying libel suit is frivolous or should be dismissed. Effective libel tourism legislation will also demand this kind of early intervention and proactive response. Anti-SLAPP protections often provide for the payment of attorney's fees to the sued parties if defamation litigation is used merely to stifle free expression, another precedent that libel tourism legislation could borrow.

I look forward to working with the subcommittee as it considers the threat of libel tourism and all appropriate means to combat it and restore the equilibrium that has been lost over the last ten years.

Exhibit A

	Public official or public figure	**Private figure on a matter of public concern**	**Private figure on a matter of private concern**
Falsity	Plaintiff bears burden of proving that statement was substantially false as a matter of federal constitutional law.[1]	Plaintiff bears burden of proving that statement was substantially false as a matter of federal constitutional law, at least where a media def-endant is involved.[2]	Burden of proof not yet decided.
Fault	Plaintiff bears burden of proving with "convincing clarity" that state-ment was made with"act-al malice," defined as knowledge of falsity or reckless disregard for truth, as a matter of federal constitu - tional law.[3]	Plaintiff bears burden of proving only negligence as a matter of federal constitut-ional law;[4] some states require proof of "actual malice" under state law.	Plaintiff bears burden of proving only negligence as a matter of federal constitutional law.[5]
Compens atory Damages	If plaintiff proves "actual malice," compensatory damages available.[6]	If plaintiff proves negligence and actual injury, com-pensatory damages available;[7] if plai-ntiff proves "actual malice," comp-ensatory damages available.[8]	If plaintiff proves negligence, comp-ensatory damages available.[9]
Punitive Damages	If plaintiff proves "actual malice," punitive damages available.[10]	Only if plaintiff proves "actual malice" are punitive damages available.[11]	If plaintiff proves negligence, punitive damages available.[12]

---

[1] *Philadelphia Newspapers Inc. v. Hepps*, 475 U.S. 767 (1986); *Masson v. New Yorker Magazine*, 501 U.S. 496 (1991). Some states require clear and convincing evidence of substantial falsity as a matter of state law.

^{2} *Hepps, supra* note 1.

^{3} *New York Times Co. v. Sullivan*, 376 U.S. 254 (1964).

^{4} *Gertz v. Robert Welch, Inc.*, 418 U.S. 323 (1974).

^{5} *Dun & Bradstreet, Inc. v. Greenmoss Builders, Inc.*, 472 U.S. 749 (1985).

^{6} *Gertz, supra* note 4.

^{7} *Gertz, supra* note 4.

^{8} *Gertz, supra* note 4.

^{9} *Dun & Bradstreet, supra* note 5.

^{10} *Gertz, supra* note 4.

^{11} *Gertz, supra* note 4.

^{12} *Dun & Bradstreet, supra* note 5.

End Notes

[1] *Reynolds v. Times Newspapers*, [1999] 4 All ER 609, [2001] 2 AC 127, [1999] 3 WLR 1010, [1999] U.K.HL 45 (permitting defendants to use a public interest defense to charges of libel, even if they could not prove the allegations were true, if they acted responsibly in publishing them).

[2] *Bose Corp. v. Consumers Union of U.S.*, 466 U.S. 485, 499 (1984).

[3] Media Law Res. Ctr. Bulletin, Issue 1, 2007 Report on Trials and Damages (Feb. 2007).

[4] Bruce D. Brown, "Write Here. Libel There. So Beware." WASH. POST., April 23, 2000, at B01

[5] Sarah Luall, "Where Suing for Libel is a National Specialty; Britain's Plaintiff-Friendly Laws Have Become a Magnet for Litigators," N.Y. TIMES, July 20, 2000.

[6] Luall, *supra* note 5.

[7] Brown, *supra* note 4.

[8] Paul Klebnikov, "Godfather of the Kremlin?" FORBES, Dec. 30, 1996.

[9] *Berezovsky v. Michaels and others*, [2000] 2 All ER 986, [2000] 1 WLR 1004, [2000] All ER (D) 643.

[10] Editor's Note, "Berezovsky versus Forbes," Forbes.com, March 6, 2003, available at http://www.forbes.com/forbes/1996/1230/5815090a_print.html.

[11] Valeria Korchagina, "Forbes Editor Klebnikov Shot Dead," MOSCOW TIMES, July 12, 2004.

[12] See www.binmahfouz.info.

[13] Doreen Carvajal, "Britain, a destination for 'libel tourism,'" INT'L HERALD TRIBUNE, Jan. 20, 2008.

[14] Carvajal, *supra* note 13.

[15] "Writ large: Are English courts stifling free speech around the world?" ECONOMIST, Jan. 10, 2009

[16] *Berezovsky, supra* note 9.

[17] *Ehrenfeld v. Bin Mahfouz*, 881 N.E.2d 830, 832 (N.Y. 2007).

[18] Carvajal, *supra* note 13.

[19] Carvajal, *supra* note 13.

[20] Carvajal, *supra* note 13.

[21] *See, e.g., Berezovsky, supra* note 9 (dismissing Forbes *forum non conveniens* argument based on the conclusion that the plaintiffs, who were not residents of the U.K., had "reputations to protect [t]here").

[22] Gary Shapiro, "Libel Suit Leads to Destruction of Books," N.Y. SUN, Aug. 2, 2007.

[23] Shapiro, *supra* note 22.

Testimony of Bruce D. Brown, Baker & Hostetler LLP, before... 69

[24] Shapiro, *supra* note 22.

[25] Scott Jaschik, "A University Press Stands Up – And Wins," INSIDE HIGHER ED, Aug. 16, 2007.

[26] Jaschik, *supra* note 25.

[27] Jaschik, *supra* note 25.

[28] Jaschik, *supra* note 25.

[29] Jaschik, *supra* note 25.

[30] Cal. Code Civ. Pro. § 425.16. SLAPP refers to "Strategic Lawsuit Against Public Participation." SLAPP suits became common in the 1980s and 1990s as real estate companies and other commercial interests sought to use libel litigation to intimidate citizen-critics who, for example, might have petitioned government officials to halt neighborhood development or mounted a publicity campaign against a local initiative. When it became evident that SLAPP suits had created a substantial chilling effect, states began to pass so-called "anti-SLAPP" laws. These laws typically allow a defendant to file a special motion to strike a libel complaint at the outset. To win an anti-SLAPP motion, the defendant must first show that the libel lawsuit is based on activity that is protected by the First Amendment. The burden then shifts to the plaintiff, who must prove that he has a reasonable probability of prevailing in the action. Many anti-SLAPP laws provide for attorney's fees and thus serve as a deterrent to the filing of frivolous libel actions.

[31] Jaschik, *supra* note 25.

[32] Jaschik, *supra* note 25.

[33] Floyd Abrams, "Be Careful What You Sue For," WALL ST. J., June 6, 2007, at A19

[34] Abrams, *supra* note 33.

[35] Arlen Specter and Joe Lieberman, "Foreign Courts Take Aim at Our Free Speech," WALL. ST. J., July 14, 2008, at A15

[36] *McFarlane v. Esquire Magazine*, 74 F.3d 1296 (D.C. Cir. 1996).

[37] *McFarlane*, *supra* note 36.

[38] Adam Cohen, "'Libel Tourism': When Freedom of Speech Takes a Holiday," N.Y. TIMES, Sept. 14, 2008.

[39] The Pearl Project, http://scs.georgetown.edu/pearlproject/.

[40] Specter and Lieberman, *supra* note 35.

[41] David Pallister, "MPs demand reform of libel laws," THE GUARDIAN, Dec. 18, 2008.

[42] Pallister, *supra* note 41.

[43] *Reynolds*, *supra* note 1.

[44] Pallister, *supra* note 41.

[45] David B. Rivkin, Jr. and Bruce D. Brown, "'Libel Tourism' Threatens Free Speech," WALL ST. J., Jan. 10, 2009

In: Libel Tourism and Foreign Libel Lawsuits   ISBN: 978-1-61209-148-8
Editor: Amy J. Brower   © 2011 Nova Science Publishers, Inc.

Chapter 5

TESTIMONY OF LAURA R. HANDMAN, DAVIS WRIGHT TREMAINE LLP, BEFORE THE SUBCOMMITTEE ON COMMERCIAL AND ADMINISTRATIVE LAW, HEARING ON "LIBEL TOURISM"

Mr. Chairman, Ranking Member Franks and Members of the Sub-committee:

QUALIFICATIONS

I am Laura R. Handman, a partner in the law firm of Davis Wright Tremaine LLP, working out of the firm's offices in New York and the District of Columbia. I am truly honored to appear before you today about an issue on which I have been on the front lines for nearly 20 years.

Following a federal district court clerkship and four years as an Assistant United States Attorney, I have devoted 25 of my 31 years of practice to representing both U.S. and British-based newspapers, magazines, broadcasters, book publishers, book sellers and online publishers. For my clients, I provide counseling prior to publication or broadcast, advising them about the legal risks arising out of the content they propose to publish or broadcast. I also represent media organizations in litigation, from complaint through trial and appeal. My representation generally involves issues of libel, privacy, copyright, trademark, reporter's privilege, newsgathering, access to information and other First Amendment content-related matters. I have been named by the British-based Chambers, the leading lawyer directory, as one of "America's Leading Business Lawyers" in National First Amendment Litigation, and was awarded the 2007 International PEN First Amendment Award from the international writers' organization. I have chaired the Communications and Media Law Committee of the Association of the Bar of the City of New York and the Media Law Committee of the Arts, Entertainment and Sports Law Section of the D.C. Bar and have served on the Governing Board of the Forum on Communications Law of the American Bar Association. I am the past President of the Defense Counsel Section of the Media Law Resource Center, the leading national organization of media defense lawyers. I am currently Co-Chair of the committee of the Council for Court Excellence drafting a Journalist's Guide to the D.C. Courts.

I have been introduced by my British counterparts to English judges as the "American lawyer who got our libel law declared repugnant." I obtained the first — and last — decisions from U.S. courts refusing to enforce British libel judgments as contrary to public policy. In *Bachchan v. India Abroad Publications, Inc.,* 585 N.Y.S.2d 661 (N.Y. Sup. Ct. 1992), an English court had imposed liability on a New York-based newspaper for a story about alleged corruption involving one of India's most prominent families. If England had had the equivalent of the actual malice standard, there would not been a judgment against the newspaper. Accordingly, the New York State court refused to enforce the British libel judgment. In *Telnikoff v. Matusevitch,* 702 A.2d 230 (Md. 1997), I argued on behalf of many leading media organizations as *amici* in Maryland's highest court in support of an American citizen who wrote a letter to the editor in response to an op-ed column in a British newspaper, suggesting the op-ed author was a "racialist" espousing a "blood test" for employment in a foreign radio service. Such a clear expression of opinion could not have been the subject of a judgment in a U.S. court. In view of these starkly outcome-determinative differences about matters of clear public concern, the New York court in 1992 and Maryland Court in 1997 refused to enforce the British libel judgments.

Because of these precedent-setting victories, I have been asked to serve as an expert on U.S. libel law in foreign libel cases in Belfast, London and Melbourne, to speak on numerous panels comparing foreign and U.S. libel law, and to write on the problem of libel tourism.[1] I have served as an expert on U.S. libel law in support of the magazine *Barron's,* published by Dow Jones & Company in two cases, *Gutnick v. Dow Jones & Co.*[2] and *Chadha &*

Testimony of Laura R. Handman, Davis Wright Tremaine LLP, before... 73

Osicom Technologies, Inc. v. Dow Jones & Co.[3] In the former, because the plaintiff was a resident of Australia, even though only five copies of the publication were sold in Victoria and just 1700 of the 550,000 international subscribers had Australia-based credit cards, jurisdiction was available in Australia. In *Chadha,* even though the London court initially found jurisdiction, because the plaintiffs were based in California with few ties to the U.K., it ultimately dismissed the case for *forum non conviens.* Unfortunately, such dismissals have been more the exception than the rule where minimal contacts and minimal publication have sufficed to keep U.S. publishers defending libel cases in British courts. I also served as an expert on behalf of Amazon.com in *Vassiliev v. Amazon.com* which involved, among other things, a review by a reader of a book sold by Amazon about the controversy over Alger Hiss. In the U.S., the website publication of a reader's comment would clearly have been protected by Section 230 of the Communications Decency Act,[4] but the U.K. has no equivalent for protection of websites for third-party comments.

BACKGROUND

Global electronic and satellite communications have erased the traditional jurisdictional boundaries that previously applied to libel law. Today, any book, article, or broadcast found online, even those published exclusively in the United States, can be subject to the libel laws of another country. As a result, publishers, journalists, authors, booksellers and other members of the American media are increasingly concerned about the practice of "libel tourism:" foreigners suing other foreigners in England or elsewhere, and using those judgments to deter authors, publishers and broadcasters from reporting on matters of public concern.[5] Libel tourism, long a tactic used by celebrities and political figures seeking to take advantage of claimant friendly libel laws, has increasingly become used to suppress legitimate reporting on public figures ranging from international financiers to business tycoons whose activities are under scrutiny.[6]

H.R. 6146 is a necessary step in the efforts to combat the effects of libel tourism. Passage of this legislation would provide protection for American authors, publishers and broadcasters from enforcement of foreign judgments that are inconsistent with the First Amendment. I have included some

74 Laura R. Handman

suggested amendments to address problems for which the current legislation may not offer sufficient redress.

Differences between U.S. and English Libel Law

Stark differences exist between U.S. and English libel law. In many ways, libel laws in the U.S. and England constitute mirror images of each other, with the burden of proof shifted to defendant in the U.K. and the plaintiff in the U.S. English libel law is essentially based on a system of strict liability — you make a mistake, you pay. As a result, many identical cases would be decided differently in the two countries. Under English law, any published statement that adversely affects an individual's reputation or the respect in which a person is held is *prima facie* defamatory.[7] The plaintiffs only burden is to establish that the allegedly defamatory statements apply to them, were published by the defendant and have a defamatory meaning.

Since allegedly defamatory statements are presumed false under British law, it is the defendant who must prove the truth or "justification" of the statements or establish another privilege to defeat the charges. If the defendant attempts to prove truth and fails, he can face an aggravated damages award. In the U.S., if the plaintiff is a public figure or public official or the statement at issue involves a matter of public concern, defendant does *not* have the burden of proving truth; the plaintiff has the burden of proving substantial falsity.[8]

While the "fair comment" exceptions under British law can save defendants from the burden of proving the truth of the underlying statement at issue, the exception provides far less protection than can be found under the comparable American law. The "fair comment" exception may apply to opinions made by the author on a matter of public interest, it must be an opinion that the author could reasonably express based on facts, and made without malice.[9] In the U.S., only statements of facts are actionable; statements that are not provable as true or false, *i.e.,* opinions, are not actionable regardless of whether a court or jury thinks they are reasonable, outlandish or harsh.[10] Statements of opinion, if the facts on which they are based are set forth fully and accurate, are not actionable, even if the speaker harbors ill will or malice.[11]

In the United States, the First Amendment provides a most important and distinct departure from England's strict liability, no fault standard. In *New York Times Co. v. Sullivan,* the U.S. Supreme Court noted that the press protections established by the American Constitution were a deliberate departure from the

British form of government.[12] At the center is our "profound national commitment to the principle that debate on public issues should be uninhibited, robust and wide-open."[13] Accordingly, the First Amendment "prohibits a public official from recovering damages for a defamatory falsehood relating to his official conduct unless he proves that the statement was made with 'actual malice' — that is, with knowledge that it was false or with reckless disregard of whether it was false or not."[14] The *Sullivan* court then went on to hold that such malice could not be presumed (376 U.S. at 283-84), that the constitutional standard requires proof having "convincing clarity" *(id.* at 285-86) and that evidence simply supporting a finding of negligence is insufficient *(id.* at 287-88). In order to succeed on a defamation claim, public figures or public officials bringing defamation actions must show that the alleged defamatory statement was made with actual malice — with the knowledge that it was false or with reckless disregard for whether or not it was false.[15]

In *Curtis Publishing Co. v. Butts,* the Supreme Court held that the principles set forth in *New York Times Co. v. Sullivan* were also applicable to the defamatory criticism of "public figures."[16] In *Gertz v. Robert Welch,* the Supreme Court held that, although the "actual malice" standard of *New York Times Co. v. Sullivan* did not extend to defamation of individual persons who were neither public officials nor public figures, the Court rejected English law of strict liability; even a private plaintiff would still be required to show some level of fault to recover damages, negligence being the bare minimum.[17]

Recent pressure by the international community against England's plaintiff- friendly libel laws have led to incremental changes in English libel law. In *Reynolds v. Times Newspapers Ltd.,* the House of Lords ruled that when the media has a legitimate duty in reporting matters of public interest, a news organization may be able to successfully defend itself against libel charges. Under the standard set forth in *Reynolds,* the criteria include the seriousness of the allegation, the steps taken to verify the information, the urgency of the matter, whether the article contained the gist of the plaintiff's side of the story, whether the comment was sought from the plaintiff, and the circumstances of the publication, including the timing [18]

In the recent case *Jameel v. Wall Street Journal Europe Sprl,*[19] a wealthy Saudi financier sued the *Wall Street Journal Europe* in London for reporting on Saudi oversight, at the request of U.S. law enforcement agencies, of certain bank accounts. Britain's House of Lords made clear that if a media defendant can show that an article or broadcast is a matter of public interest and a product of "responsible journalism," a plaintiff cannot recover libel damages. Although *Jameel* set forth a new standard for British courts to apply to the activities of American journalists or publishers who might be sued in the U.K., the protections afforded under *Jameel* are still less than those provided to publishers and authors in the U.S. The British standard of "responsible journalism" would seem to allow the judge to evaluate, with 20/20 hindsight, the fairness of the journalism; the actual malice standard sets a much higher bar, reaching only what is tantamount to deliberate falsehoods a subjective bad faith test. Failure to adequately investigate is *not* the test for actual malice.[20]

The English system differs from the American system in other important ways. In England, the statute of limitations runs from whenever a magazine, book, newspaper, or Internet posting is available. In the United States, the statute of limitations generally begins to run from the first publication of the statement, even if the publication stays on sale or the posting stays up on the Internet.[21] With regard to jurisdiction, a few hits on a website on the Internet in Great Britain may be enough to give Commonwealth courts jurisdiction to hear the plaintiff's libel case, even if the content or the web server is physically located in another country.[22] Contrast this to the United States, where in *Young v. New Haven Advocate,* the Fourth Circuit held that an out of state defendant's Internet activity must be expressly targeted at or directed to the forum state to establish the minimum contacts necessary to support the exercise of personal jurisdiction over defendant by district court in the forum state.[23] In the U.S., Internet service providers are immune from liability for speech by third parties posted on their websites.[24] In Britain, no such immunity exists. Under British law, a libel plaintiff can obtain an injunction against publication of the defamatory material.[25] In the U.S., such an injunction would be deemed an illegal prior restraint.[26]

Another stark difference between the English and American systems emerges around the issue of attorneys fees. In England, the courts allow fee shifting. Under fee shifting, the losing party must bear all of the costs associated with the litigation, including their own. This substantially increases the cost of litigation as most libel cases in the Great Britain require multiple attorneys. Under the "American rule," attorneys' fees are not awarded to the prevailing party unless authorized by law. State anti-SLAPP statutes are one such provision for fees to a prevailing libel defendant.[27]

The Dangers of Libel Tourism

The term "libel tourism" refers to what essentially amounts to international forum shopping. Often, the claimant will seek out friendly libel laws of foreign jurisdictions to bring claims against members of the American media that would be barred (or far more difficult to bring) under American law.[28] This practice permits the "libel tourist" to avoid the rigorous protections afforded to speech and press under American law by filing a claim against a publisher or an author in a country with far fewer protections for such defendants.

Libel tourism is a growing trend. Increasingly, individuals who claim to be maligned by American publications or authors are turning to courts overseas to try their claims. With laws that favor plaintiffs, countries like Great Britain are becoming tourist destinations for defamation claims.[29] Often, this occurs even when the foreign jurisdiction has virtually no legitimate connection to the challenged publication or to the claimant. *Forbes* is currently facing lawsuits in Ireland, Northern Ireland and England for a story published in its domestic edition about the North Pole. *The Washington Times* is currently facing a claim by an international businessman, a resident of London, for an article about an unpublished Pentagon report into the award of cell phone contracts in Iraq. No hard copies of *The Washington Times* were sold in the U.K. and there were only forty or so hits on the newspaper's website. The following are just a few recent examples highlighting the threats posed by libel tourism actions:

Celebrities: Celebrities, particularly Americans, are some of the most frequent libel tourists. In 2007, celebrities accounted for a third of all libel actions brought in England and Wales based on figures released by British legal publishers Sweet and Maxwell.[30] Advised that it is easier to win defamation and privacy claims in the United Kingdom than it is in the United States, the numbers of American celebrities who are bringing such actions in the United Kingdom is increasing.[31] Actor Harrison Ford has consulted a solicitor in Belfast over claims in United States newspapers relating to the reprisal of his role in the most recent Indiana Jones movie, *The Kingdom of the Crystal Skull.*[32] *The National Enquirer* is frequently visited by libel tourists — including Britney Spears, U.S. film producer Steve Bing, Jennifer Lopez and Marc Anthony.[33] In 2005, *The National Enquirer* cut off access to British viewers of its website based on a settlement with American actress Cameron Diaz over a story that Diaz cheated on Justin Timberlake.[34] Although the story did not appear in the U.K. version of the *Enquirer,* Diaz was able to sue because the story was viewed 279 times from U.K. Internet addresses.[35]

French citizen and Oscar-winning director Roman Polanski won £50,000 in damages against U.S.-based Conde Nast after it was published in the 2002

July edition of *Vanity Fair* that he tried to seduce a Swedish model on his way to California for Sharon Tate's funeral, claiming that he told the model he could make her "another Sharon Tate."[36] In granting Polanski, a native of France and a fugitive from the American justice system, permission to sue *in absentia* in a London court and appear in the civil proceedings via video link from Paris, the House of Lords held that the English judicial system did not preclude a fugitive from U.S. justice from bringing defamation proceedings in England.[37]

International businessmen: In 1989, American oil magnate Armand Hammer instituted a libel suit in London in connection with an unauthorized biography that was distributed primarily in the United States.[38] The late publisher Robert Maxwell sued *The New Republic* in Britain where less than 35 copies of the publication circulated. In 1997, Texas oil magnate Oscar Wyatt sued *Forbes* in London for libel based on an article titled: "Saddam's Pal Oscar." Even though the article in question made no mention of London, Wyatt chose London as a forum based on the frequency of his trips to London and the fact that his son was the Duchess of York's infamous toe-sucking paramour.[39] In 1997, California businessman Parvindar Chadha sued Dow Jones in London based on an article published in Barrons on his company (located in California) despite the fact that less than .4% of Barron's circulation is in the U.K.[40] In 2002, *New Yorker* investigative reporter Seymour Hersh wrote a series of articles highly critical of Richard Perle, one of President George Bush's most influential advisors. Perle vowed to sue Hersh in London but ultimately failed to follow through.[41] Sheik Khalid bin Mahfouz has been a frequent user of England's libel laws. In addition to the lawsuit filed against author Rachel Ehrenfeld, bin Mahfouz has filed multiple libel lawsuits in England, targeting any media organization that has ever printed any allegations that the bin Mahfouz family has connections to terrorism.[42]

In 1997, Russian oligarch Boris Berezovsky sued *Forbes* for libel in the London High Court over an article that appeared in the domestic version of *Forbes'* publication. Of the more than 780,000 copies of the magazine distributed, fewer than 6,000 readers likely saw the magazine in England and Wales (1,915 copies were circulated through newsstands and subscriptions, the remainder through viewing on the Internet).[43] Lord Hoffman upheld Berezovsky's right to sue *Forbes* in London in the House of Lords, holding that London should provide a forum for libel litigants from around the world, "I do not have to decide whether Russia or America is more appropriate *inter*

Testimony of Laura R. Handman, Davis Wright Tremaine LLP, before... 79

se. I merely have to decide whether there is some other forum where substantial justice can be done [...]. If a plaintiff is libeled in this country, *prima facie,* he should be allowed to bring his claim here where the publication is."[44]

Although British courts are beginning to recognize important protections for libel defendants, even Members of Parliament acknowledge international furor over the practice of libel tourism. In remarks given before the House of Commons on December 17, 2008 by The Rt Hon. Dennis MacShane MP, MacShane acknowledged the problem of libel tourism and the role that it is playing in the assault on freedom of information and called for Parliament to take action on the issue, noting that it was "unbelievable that the state legislators of New York and Illinois, and Congress itself, are having to pass Bills to stop British courts seeking to fine and punish American journalist and writers for publishing books and articles that may be freely read in the United States but which a British judge has decided are offensive to wealthy foreigners who can hire lawyers in Britain to persuade a British court to become a new Soviet-style organ of censorship against freedom of expression."[45]

Non Enforcement of British Libel Judgments by U.S. Courts

No federal law or standard exists for the recognition and enforcement of foreign country judgments in the United States.[46] While judgments of sister states are regulated by the Full Faith and Credit Clause of the U.S. Constitution, foreign country judgments are not.[47] The United States is not currently a party to any treaties or international agreements governing the recognition and enforcement of judgments rendered by the courts.[48] Congress has the authority to enact legislation that would prohibit the recognition and enforcement of foreign declaratory judgments if those judgments are inconsistent with the First Amendment.

I was involved in the only two decisions where American courts have refused to enforce English libel judgments on the broad ground that England's libel laws are repugnant to the fundamental protections afforded by the First Amendment and state constitutional law.[49]

Bachchan v. India Abroad

In *Bachchan v. India Abroad Publications, Inc., India Abroad,* a small New York based publication reported that, according to Sweden's leading newspaper *Dagens Nyheter ("DN")*, kickbacks from arms sales to the Indian government had been deposited into the Swiss bank account of Indian national Ajitabh Bachchan. Bachchan, a close friend of then-Prime Minister Rajiv Ghandi, also served as business manager to his brother, Amitabh Bachchan, who at the time was India's leading Bollywood star. As a result, Ajitabh Bachchan was a well known public figure to Indians around the world. Bachchan sued both *DN* and *India Abroad* for libel in England. Although *India Abroad* was distributed overwhelmingly in the United States, Bachchan (an Indian national claiming London residency) sued *India Abroad* for libel in England based on distribution of 1,000 copies of a wire version of the *India Abroad* story.[50] Bachchan and *DN* (the original source of the story) subsequently entered into a settlement in which *DN* apologized, saying that it had been the "unwitting victim of a story planted by some unscrupulous...persons in India." Even though *India Abroad* (as well as every other major Indian newspaper and wire service) had relied in good faith on *DN's* reporting of the story, and even though Bachchan was a public figure, he was not required to prove any fault by *India Abroad* (not even negligence) under English common law. Instead, *India Abroad* was held strictly liable in England to the tune of E40,000 for publishing a story based on another paper's "unwitting" error.

Bachchan had considerably less luck enforcing his judgment in the United States. Fresh off his victory in the English court system, Bachchan subsequently instituted a proceeding in a New York state trial court to enforce his English award against *India Abroad.* I was retained by the late Gopal Raju to represent *India Abroad* in the New York proceeding. Finding English libel law fundamentally at odds with First Amendment jurisprudence, the court declined enforcement on the public policy grounds that the enforcement of a British libel judgment in the United States is repugnant to American public policy:

> *It is true that England and the United States share many common law principles of law. Nonetheless, a significant difference between the two jurisdictions lies in England's lack of equivalent to the First Amendment. The protection to free speech and the press embodied in [the first amendment] would be seriously jeopardized by entry of foreign libel judgments pursuant to standards deemed appropriate in England but considered antithetical to the protections afforded to the press by the U.S. Constitution.[51]*

Had this case been brought in an American court, the case would have been dismissed at the outset on the grounds that *India Abroad* had relied on a reputable news organization. [52]

Matusevitch v. Telnikoff

The Maryland high court reached a similar conclusion *in Matusevitch v. Telnikoff*. In *Telnikoff*,[53] Soviet émigré turned English citizen Vladimir Ivanovich Telnikoff complained in an op-ed published in London's *Daily Telegraph* that the BBC's Russian Service employed too many "Russian-speaking national minorities" and not enough of "those who associate themselves ethnically, spiritually or religiously with the Russian people." This op-ed prompted an angry letter to the editor (also published in the *Telegraph)* from Soviet Jewish émigré Vladimir Matusevitch who protested that Telnikoff was advocating a "switch from professional testing to a blood test" and was stressing a "racialist recipe" under which "no matter how high the standards 'of ethnically alien' people, they should be dismissed." [54] The letter written by Matusevitch, an American citizen by birth who, at the time, was living in London, working for Radio Free Europe, was a classic example of the heated hyperbole uttered in the course of public debate that is protected by the First Amendment in this country as non-actionable opinion. In England, however, such discourse was not protected, and Telnikoff ultimately secured a £240,000 pound award against Matusetivch from a jury, which found that that Matusevitch's letter to the editor conveyed the "fact" that Telnikoff was a racialist.

After the decision, Matusevitch returned to the United States, settling in Maryland. When Telnikoff sought to enforce his English judgment against him in the U.S., Matusevitch instituted a civil rights action in federal district court in Washington, D.C. in this action. I represented major American media as *amici* at every level of the U.S. proceedings. The District Court found that the British award was repugnant to Maryland public policy and First Amendment principles. After Telnikoff appealed the district court's decision, the D.C. Circuit certified to Maryland's highest court the question of whether recognition of Telnikoff's English libel judgment would contravene the public policy of the state of Maryland. Reaching a conclusion similar to that of the *India Abroad* court, the Maryland Court of Appeals, by a vote of 6 to 1, broadly held that, "[a]t heart of the First Amendment... is the recognition of the fundamental importance of the free flow of ideas and opinions on matters of public interest and concern... the importance of that free flow of ideas and opinions on matters ofpublic concern precludes Maryland recognition of Telnikoff's English libel judgment."[55]

In *India Abroad* and *Telnikoff,* state courts in New York and Maryland held that recognition of foreign libel judgments in the United States contravened the public policy of not only New York and Maryland, but also the United States. In *India Abroad,* the court went one step further and stated that not only would the court not recognize or enforce Bachchan's libel judgment against *India Abroad,* the court had a constitutional obligation not to: "[i]f, as claimed by defendant, the public policy to which the foreign judgment is repugnant is embodied in the First Amendment to the United States Constitution or the free speech guaranty of the Constitution of this State, the refusal to recognize the judgment should be, and is deemed to be, 'constitutional mandatory.'"[56]

Although *India Abroad* and *Telnikoff* set the precedent that English libel laws were repugnant to the fundamental speech and press protections afforded by the First Amendment and state press laws, more recent efforts to have foreign decisions declared unenforceable have been unsuccessful.[57] The leading case involves Rachel Ehrenfeld who was sued by bin Mahfouz for libel in England based on allegations Ehrenfeld made in her book, *Funding Evil: How Terrorism is Financed—and How to Stop It.* After Ehrenfeld did not appear in the English case, the English court issued a default judgment against her. Bin Mahfouz did not come to the U.S. to enforce the judgment; he instead posted the British judgment on his website as a warning to future authors and reporters. Immediately after the judgment was received, Ehrenfeld filed a complaint in the Southern District of New York seeking a declaration under the Declaratory Judgment Act, 28 U.S.C. § 2201, asking the court to declare that (1) bin Mahfouz could not prevail on a libel claim against Ehrenfeld under the laws of New York and the United States; and (2) the judgment in the English case was not enforceable in the United States on constitutional and public policy grounds. Following dismissal on jurisdictional grounds, the Second Circuit certified the jurisdictional question to the New York Court of Appeals.

Answering the question certified to it by the Court of Appeals for the Second Circuit, the Court of Appeals found that the "[t]he mere receipt by a non-resident of a benefit or profit from a contract performed by others in New York is clearly not an act to confer jurisdiction under our long-arm statute."[58] According to the Court of Appeals, bin Mahfouz's contacts with Ehrenfeld were necessary to receive the benefit of his judgment. The Court of Appeals acknowledged the problem of libel tourism, but stated that "however pernicious the effect of this practice may be, our duty here is to determine whether [bin Mahfouz]'s New York contacts establish a proper basis for jurisdiction" and bin Mahfouz's contacts did not meet that threshold. Plaintiff's arguments regarding the enlargement of CPLR 302(a)(1) to confer jurisdiction upon "libel tourists" must be directed to the legislature.

New York and Illinois responded to the Ehrenfeld Court's call to act by passing legislation which would provide authors, publishers and media outlets in those states protection from threats of local enforcement of libel tourism. Illinois and New York have passed laws that give residents the right to file a complaint in the courts of those states to have foreign libel judgments declared unenforceable if issued by courts where free- speech standards are lower than those in the United States.[59] These extend the state's long arm jurisdiction to any person who obtains a judgment in a defamation proceeding outside the United States.

Impact on Publishing Decisions

Without the passage of this legislation, libel tourism threatens to have a significant "chilling effect" on the expressive activities of American authors, publishers, media organizations and non-governmental organizations. The Internet age of global satellite and electronic communications has produced a world without borders. Today, any book, article, television newscast or blogpost available online, even one published exclusively in another country, can ostensibly be subject to the libel law of a foreign jurisdiction. U.S. publishers my firm represents now routinely get letters on behalf of U.S.-based celebrities and businessmen simultaneously from both U.S. and British law firms threatening lawsuits in the United Kingdom if the U.S. publisher decides to publish an article the celebrity feels is defamatory. If the publication has already been published, confronted with the possibility of a claim in the U.K. where the law so favors the plaintiff, U.S. publishers are settling claims that would never succeed in the U.S. With the enormous economic constraints currently faced by newspapers and magazines, they cannot possibly incur the risk. Fear of a lawsuit by members of the Saudi Royal Family prevented publication in the United Kingdom of *House of Bush, House of Saud* by Craig Unger and *While America Slept: The Failure to Prevent 9-11,* by Gerald Posner, even though both books were cleared for publication and published in the United States and the information was of equal importance to a worldwide, not just domestic, audience.[60]

In Britain, the losing party must bear the fees of the prevailing party, as well as his own. The fees often far exceed by several multiples any damages

84 Laura R. Handman

award, since each party in the typical libel matter is represented by two banisters and two solicitors, at a minimum, and the fees typically run to 1 million dollars for each side.[61] Since the law so favors the plaintiff, the likelihood of a substantial fee award to the prevailing plaintiff only magnifies the burden faced by any defendant sued in a U.K. court. This is further compounded by the fact that jurisdiction lies wherever the publication is found. *Forbes* magazine is facing three separate claims arising out of the same article (about a marathon in the North Pole) published in its U.S. edition, brought in Ireland, Northern Ireland and England. The Belfast-based solicitor who brought the triple play has bragged to Dublin's *Sunday Tribune:* "Facing three separate legal costs and possible damages can be effective in terms of concentrating a publisher's mind and encouraging early settlement."[62]

Legislative Proposal

H.R. 6146 is a strong measure effectively codifying on a federal level the two state courts decisions in *Bachchan* and *Telnikoffwhich* applied the provisions of the Uniform Foreign Money Judgments Recognition Act in effect at the time. The legislation sponsored by Chairman Cohen and passed by the House of Representatives in the 110th Congress last September is a much needed step toward ending the practice of forum-shopping by U.S. celebrities, foreign business tycoons, those suspected of supporting terrorism, or anyone seeking laws that lack the protections afforded the First Amendment to wield against U.S.-based authors, publishers, broadcasters and web publishers. By focusing on actions by public figures or matters of public concern, the legislation reaches public speech at the core of the First Amendment.

While it is a most important first step, there are a number of concerns that the legislation, as valuable as it is, leaves unaddressed. Many of the larger news organizations have assets overseas against which foreign libel judgments can be enforced. As a result, the successful overseas libel plaintiff need not come to the U.S. to enforce an otherwise unenforceable judgment against a larger media entity.

Even if there are no assets overseas, the successful libel plaintiff may choose to avoid the obstacles of enforcement in the U.S. but nonetheless use the judgment of the foreign court to discourage any further reporting about the controversy. Many media organizations will be fearful of publishing in face of a libel verdict that holds that the statements are not true, even if that verdict is the product of laws that would not have been applied in the U.S. and, even worse, the product of a process where the U.S.-based author or publisher did not appear to defend. That is, indeed, what happened in the *Ehrenfeld* case. Mr. bin Mahfouz posted his verdicts on his website as a warning sign to discourage future reporting. It has had the predictable effect, resulting in Cambridge University Press destroying its book, *Alms for Jihad,* on the subject.[63]

Finally, the absence of the various protections for speech is magnified several fold by fee-shifting that is standard in the U.K. for a prevailing party but is contrary to the American rule. The fees are typically several multiples of any verdict and, of course, the fees are times two since the losing party must bear his own as well as those of the prevailing parties!

To address these concerns, I suggest one or more of the following additions to the current legislation:

1. Add a remedy for declaratory judgment. This remedy could be added without expanding the jurisdictional due process constraints that would normally apply. Even with the due process constraints, libel plaintiffs who file overseas but are based in the U.S., have substantial contacts in the U.S., or take actions making suit in the U.S. foreseeable, would be subject to a declaratory judgment action in the U.S., even if they do not come to the U.S. to enforce the judgment.
2. Add an award of fees and costs to the party who has been sued in an overseas action and who prevails in the domestic court, so that they can recoup all reasonable attorney's fees and costs, including those incurred in connection with the overseas action. This would be akin to the fee provisions of anti-SLAPP statutes that have been passed in 25 states to discourage suits that are intended to burden speech.[64]
3. Require that a bond be posted by the party seeking to enforce the overseas judgment.

CONCLUSION

The judges in *Bachchan* and *Matusevitch* and the legislatures in New York and Illinois have recognized the dangers posed by enforcement of foreign judgments inconsistent with the principles secured by the First Amendment. The passage of H.R. 6146 by Congress is a necessary step to

86 Laura R. Handman

restore to American authors, publishers, booksellers and other members of the media the speech rights that they have long enjoyed in this country.

I thank you for the opportunity to speak to you today and look forward to answering the questions of the Committee and working with the Committee in the future on this legislation.

End Notes

[1] *"Bachchan v. India Abroad:* Non Recognition of British Libel Judgments: The American Revolution Revisited," *Communications Lawyer,* a publication of the ABA, Fall 1992 (with Robert D. Balin).

[2] [2002] HCA 56, 210 C.L.R. 575 (Austl.).

[3] [1999] E.M.L.R. 724, [1999] I.L.Pr. 829, [1999] EWCA Civ 1415.

[4] 47 U.S.C. § 230; *Schnieder v. Amazon.com, Inc.,* 31 P.3d 37 (Wash. Ct. App. 2001) (Amazon.com not liable for reader's comment).

[5] Rachel Donadio, *Libel Without Borders,* N.Y. Times, Oct. 7, 2007, *http://www.nytimes.com/2007/10/07/books/review/Donadio-t.html?pagewanted=1&_r=2.*

[6] Michael Peel & Megan Murphy, *English Courts In The Dock On "Libel Tourism,"* Financial Times, Apr. 2, 2008, *http://us.ft.com/ftgateway/superpage.ft?news_id=fto040120082148266717.*

[7] Rodney A. Smolla, *Law of Defamation* § 1.9 (2d ed. 1999).

[8] In *Philadelphia Newspapers v. Hepps,* 475 U.S. 767, 768-69 (1986), the Supreme Court held that "where a newspaper publishes speech of public concern, a private-figure plaintiff cannot recover damages [in a defamation action] without also showing that the statements at issue are false."

[9] Heather Maly, *Publish At Your Own Risk Or Don't Publish At All: Forum Shopping Trends In Libel Litigation Leave The First Amendment Un-Guaranteed,* 14 J.L. & Pol'y 883, 901 (2006).

[m] *Milkovich v. Lorain Journal Co.,* 497 U.S. 1, 19-20 (1990).

[11] *Id.* at 20 ("a statement of opinion relating to matters of public concern which does not contain a provably false factual connotation will receive full constitutional protection").

[12] *New York Times Co. v. Sullivan,* 376 U.S. 254, 274 (1964).

[13] *Id* at 270.

[14] *Id* at 279-80.

[15] *Sullivan,* 376 U.S. at 279-80.

[16] 388 U.S. 130 (1967).

[17] 418 U.S. 323, 347 (1974).

[18] *Reynolds v. Times Newspapers Ltd,* [1999] 4 All E.R. 609, [2001] 2 A.C. 127, [1999] UKHL 45.

[19] *Jameel v. Wall Street Journal Europe Sprl,* [2007] 1 A.C. 359, [2006] 4 All E.R. 1279, [2006] UKHL 44. [2°] *St. Amant v. Thompson,* 390 U.S. 727 (1968).

[21] Judge Robert Sack, *Sack on Defamation,* § 7.2 (3d ed. 2007).

[22] *Celebrity Settles U.K. Libel Suit with National Enquirer,* News Media Update, Reporters Committee for a Free Press, Mar. 5, 2007, *http://vvvvwxcfp/news/200710305-lib.celebr.html.*

[23] *Young v. New Haven Advocate,* 315 F.3d 256, 262 (4th Cir. 2002) (reversing and dismissing for lack of jurisdiction libel claims brought in Virginia against *The Hartford Courant* and *The New Haven Advocate).*

Testimony of Laura R. Handman, Davis Wright Tremaine LLP, before... 87

[24] Under the Communications Decency Act, 47 U.S.C. § 230, Internet service providers are immune from liability based on content created by a third party.

[25] *See* http://www.binmahfouzinfo/news_2005053.html.

[26] Sack, *Sack on Defamation,* § 10.6.1.

[27] Cal. Civ. Proc. Code § 425.16.

[28] Michael Isikoff & Mark Hosenball, *Terror Watch: Libel Tourism,* Newsweek, Oct. 22, 2003, http://www.newsweek.com/id/61629.

[29] *See* Jack Schafer, *Richard Perle Libel Watch Week 2,* Slate, Mar. 19, 2003, *http://www.slate.com/id/2080384.* England is not the only jurisdiction with laws that favor the plaintiff in defamation actions. Singapore has been called a "libel paradise" and New Zealand and Kyrgyzstan are also noted for being friendly to plaintiffs. However, given the plaintiff friendly legal environment in London, its proximity to the United States and the exposure of many media companies to the English market, England remains a favored destination for plaintiffs looking to engage in libel tourism.

[30] Robert Verkaik, *London Becomes Dafamation Capital for World's Celebrities,* The Independent, Oct. 13, 2008, http://www.independent.co.u1c/news/uldhome-news/london-becomes-defamation-

[31] *Id.*

[32] Robert Verkaik, *Invasion of the Libel Tourists,* The Independent, Aug. 21, 2008, http://www.independent.co.uk/news/u1c/home-news/invasion-of-the-libel-tourists-904111.html.

[33] *Id*

[34] Aline van Duyn, *Plug Pulled in UK over Libel Stance,* Financial Times, Mar. 17, 2007.

[35] *Id*

[36] Claire Cozens, *Polanski Wins Libel Case Against Vanity Fair,* The Guardian, July 22, 2005, http://www.guardian

[37] *See Polanski v. Conde Nast Publ'ns Ltd.,* [2005] 1 All E.R. 945, [2005] UKHL 10.

[38] Handman & Balin, *supra* note 1.

[39] Laura R. Handman & Robert Balin, *"It's a Small World After All: Emerging Protections for the U.S. Media Sued in England, http://www.dvvt.com/related_links/adv_bulletins/CMIT FALL1998USMedia.htm.*

[40] *Chadha v. Dow Jones & Co.,* slip op. (High Ct. of Justice, Queen's Bench Division, 1997).

[41] Jack Schafer, *Richard Perle Libel Watch — the Finale,"* Slate, Mar. 15, 2004, http:/www.slate.com/2097180.

[42] *See* http://www.binmahfouz.info.

[43] Avi Bell, *Libel Tourism: International Forum Shopping For Defamation Claims,* Global Law Forum at 17 (2008), http://wvvw.globallawforum/org/UserFiles/puzzle22New(1).pdf.

[44] *Id* at 18.

[45] Remarks of the Rt. Hon. Dennis MacShane (Statement of MacShane before Parliament on Libel Tourism), Dec. 17, 2008, *http://www.publications.parliament.uk/pa/c m200809/cmhansra/cm081217/* halltext/81217h0001.htm. In his remarks, MacShane stated that, "[a]s in the 18th century, the British establishment is seeking to silence Americans who want to reveal the truth about the murkier goings-on in our independent world. The practice of libel tourism as it is known - the willingness of British courts to allow wealthy foreigners who do not live here to attack publications who have no connection with Britain — is now an international scandal. It shames Britian and makes a mockery of the idea that Britian is a protector of core democratic freedoms. Libel tourism sounds innocuous, but underneath that banal phrase is a major assault on freedom of information, which in today's complex world is more necessary than ever."

[46] A proposed federal statute creating a uniform national rule for enforcement of foreign country judgments has been adopted by the American Law Institute (ALI). *See* American Law Institute, Recognition and Enforcement of Foreign Judgments: Analysis and Proposed Federal Statute; Adopted and Promulgated by the American Law Institute, May 15, 2005

(2006),http://www.silha.umn.edu/Bulletin/Fall%202008%20
Bulletin/House%20Passes%20Libel%20Tourism%20Bill;%20Illinois%20Enacts%20Its%2
0Own%20Law. html.

[47] *Hilton v. Guyot,* 159 U.S. 113, 181-82 (1895).

[48] The Hague Convention on Choice Agreements would require Convention parties to recognize, with some exceptions, judgments rendered by a court in another signatory country that was designated in a choice of court agreement between litigants. The Convention would likely apply to defamation judgments. The United States has not yet ratified the Convention, which to date has not entered into force.

[49] *Bachchan v. India Abroad Publ'ns, Inc.,* 585 N.Y.S.2d 661 (N.Y. Sup. Ct. 1992) and *Matusevitch v. Telnikoff,* 702 A.2d 230 (Md. 1997).

[50] This number represented approximately 2% of the total of copies of *India Abroad* distributed. Ninety- one point two percent (91.2%) of the copies were distributed in the United States. *India Abroad* had a U.K. subsidiary and a London office.

[51] *India Abroad,* 585 N.Y.S.2d at 684.

[52] Sack, *Sack on Defamation, § 7.3.*

[53] *Telnikoff,* 702 A.2d at 251.

[54] *Id* at 233.

[55] *Telnikoff* 702 A. 2d at 251.

[56] *India Abroad,* 585 N.Y.S.2d at 662.

[57] *Ehrenfeld v. Bin Mahfouz,* No. 06-2228, 2007 WL 1662062 (2d Cir. June 8, 2007). In addition, other attempts to use the Declaratory Judgment Act to prevent recognition of U.K. libel judgments has proved unsuccessful on jurisdictional grounds. *See Dow Jones & Co. v. Harrods Ltd.,* 346 F.3d 357 (2d Cir. 2003) (Dow Jones attempt to bar Harrod's from filing a libel lawsuit in U.K. was dismissed on grounds that the Court did not have personal or subject matter jurisdiction.); *Yahoo! v. La Ligue Contre Le Racisme Et L'Antisemitisme,* 433 F.3d 1199 (9th Cir. 2006) (en banc) (9th Circuit sitting en banc dismisses for jurisdictional reasons *Yahoo!* request for declaratory order preventing enforcement of French Court's order to ISP to block French citizen's access to Nazi material displayed or offered on *Yahoo's* United States site.)

[58] *Ehrenfeld v. Bin Mahfouz,* 881 N.E.2d 830 (N.Y. 2007).

[59] *See* Governor Paterson Signs Legislation Protecting New Yorkers Against Infringement Of First Amendment Rights By Foreign Libel Judgments, May 1, 2008, *http://ww w.ny.gov/governor* 735 Ill. Comp. Stat. 5/2-209.

[60] Ron Chepesiuk, *Libel Tourism Chills US-Based Investigative Journalism,* The Daily Star, Apr. 30, 2004, http://www.thedailystar.net/2004/04/30/d404301501109.htm.

[61] *Writ Large,* The Economist, Jan. 8, 2009, http ://www. economist. com/worl d/international/displaystory. cfm?story_id=12903058.

[62] Suzanne Breen, *She's Just Jenny from the H-Blocks to Lawyer Tweed,* Sunday Trib., Aug. 31, 2008, *http://www.tribune.ie/news/international/article/2008/aug/3 l/shes-just-jenny-from-the-h-blocks-to-lawyertweed/.*

[63] *See* http://www.binmahfouz.ufo/news_20070730.html. Bin Mahfouz sued Cambridge University Press for libel relating to allegations contained in *Alms for Jihad.* Rather than go to trial, Cambridge University decided to settle, agreeing to pulp all unsold copies of the book.

[64] We count 25 states and one territory with anti-SLAPP statutes: Arizona, Arkansas, California, Delaware, Florida, Georgia, Hawaii, Illinois, Indiana, Louisiana, Maine, Maryland, Massachusetts, Minnesota, Missouri, Nebraska, Nevada, New Mexico, New York, Oregon, Pennsylvania, Rhode Island, Tennessee, Utah, Washington and Guam. Adapting the structure from California's Anti-SLAPP Statute, the party resisting a foreign libel judgment would be able to make a special motion within 60 days requiring the party seeking to enforce the judgment to make *a prima facie* showing that the judgment was consistent with the First Amendment. If the party resisting enforcement were successful, that party would

be awarded attorney's fees and costs. If the movant was unsuccessful, the party seeking to enforce the judgment would only be awarded fees if the motion were frivolous.

In: Libel Tourism and Foreign Libel Lawsuits ISBN: 978-1-61209-148-8
Editor: Amy J. Brower © 2011 Nova Science Publishers, Inc.

Chapter 6

STATEMENT OF PROFESSOR LINDA J. SILBERMAN, MARTIN LIPTON PROFESSOR OF LAW, NEW YORK UNIVERSITY SCHOOL OF LAW, BEFORE THE SUBCOMMITTEE ON COMMERCIAL AND ADMINISTRATIVE LAW, HEARING ON "LIBEL TOURISM"

I am Professor Linda Silberman, and I am the Martin Lipton Professor of Law at New York University School of Law, where I have been teaching and writing about Civil Procedure, Conflict of Laws, Comparative Civil Procedure, and Private International Law for over 35 years. With respect to the particular issue of the recognition of foreign country judgments on which this hearing focuses, I was Co-Reporter, along with my colleague Professor Andreas Lowenfeld, of the recently completed (in 2006) American Law Institute Project entitled "Recognition and Enforcement of Foreign Judgments: Analysis and Proposed Federal Statute", which offers a comprehensive proposal for a federal statute governing the recognition and enforcement of foreign country judgments. The ALI Project represents the position of the American Law Institute, but this written testimony and my statements today represent only my own views and not those of the Institute or of any group.

Before turning to the particular problem of "libel tourism", I think it is useful to say a word about the law in the United States relating to the recognition and enforcement of foreign country judgments. Interestingly, the United States has no bilateral or multinational treaty dealing with the recognition or enforcement of foreign judgments. And unlike the full faith and credit obligation which is owed to domestic sister state judgments, foreign country judgments are not subject to the constitutional or statutory full faith and credit obligation. Even more curious, I think, is the fact that the subject of recognition and enforcement of foreign country judgments in the United States has been treated as a matter of state law. As a result, the judgment of an English or German or Japanese court might be recognized and enforced in Texas, but not in Arkansas, in Pennsylvania but not in New York. In my view, and in the only case in which the Supreme Court of the United States has addressed the subject,[1] a foreign country judgment presented in the United States for recognition or enforcement is an aspect of the relations between the United States and the foreign state, even if the particular controversy involves the rights of private parties. Accordingly, recognition and enforcement of foreign judgments is and ought to be a matter of national federal concern. However, a curious history has left the law of recognition and enforcement of foreign country judgments in the hands of the states,[2] and while a number of (but not all) states have adopted the Uniform Foreign Money-Judgments Recognition Act, even the adoptions are not uniform. [3] For example, some states have included a requirement of reciprocity – that is, the requirement that if a foreign country judgment is to be recognized and enforced in the United States, the foreign country must also respect a United States judgment in similar circumstances. Other states have no such requirement. Moreover, the highest court of each state is the final interpreter of the provisions of its Act, and as a result the Uniform Act is not uniform. These differences in state laws create a situation where a foreign country judgment may be enforced in one state and not in another. Thus, there is no single, uniform American law to govern the recognition and enforcement of foreign judgments.

I applaud the Committee for addressing the subject of recognition and enforcement of foreign country judgments at the national level. Ideally, Congress would identify the principles that guide recognition and enforcement of foreign country judgments and would legislate a national solution in the form of a coherent federal statute. That is indeed the proposal of the American Law Institute Project, which offers a framework for a comprehensive federal statute on the subject of recognition and enforcement of foreign country judgments, and a proposal to which I would urge this Committee to give serious consideration.

Let me now turn to the particular problem of foreign libel judgments in which a foreign court applies a law that is less protective of speech than would be required under United States law, in particular, the First Amendment. The issue may become a matter for the courts of the United States in one of two ways. The successful plaintiff may seek to enforce the foreign judgment in the United States.[4] Or, as several recent cases have illustrated, the defendant against whom the foreign judgment is rendered may seek a declaration in a U.S. court that the judgment should not be recognized, at least in the United States.[5] Under existing law in every state of the United States --- and indeed under principles adopted by almost every country[6] – a foreign country judgment may be refused recognition on grounds that the judgment is repugnant to the public policy of the state asked to recognize or enforce the judgment.[7] And under existing state law, courts in the United States have refused to recognize foreign libel judgments when they believe First Amendment principles have been violated. Therefore, H.R. 6146, which provides that a domestic court "shall not recognize or enforce a foreign judgment for defamation that is based upon a publication concerning a public figure or a matter of public concern unless the domestic court determines that the foreign judgment is consistent with the first amendment to the Constitution of the United States" does not really change existing law. The provision in H.R. 6146 is more precise than the general "public policy" exception, and it does make clear that as a *national* matter First Amendment concerns trump the more general policy of recognizing and enforcing foreign country judgments. But courts in the United States already consistently invoke First Amendment values in determining whether to deny recognition and enforcement of foreign judgments on grounds of public policy.[8] Indeed, courts have invoked *state* policy as well as federal policy, and thus it may be necessary to clarify that the federal policy here is preemptive.[9]

More critically perhaps, the proposed provision does not solve the private international law aspects of the proper scope for "public policy" when that exception is invoked. Specifically, it does not distinguish situations where it would be appropriate for courts in the United States to recognize and enforce a foreign libel judgment from those where recognition and enforcement should be refused. Let me illustrate with the example of the *Telnikoff v. Matusevitch* case.[10] There, a libel judgment was obtained by one resident of England (Telnikoff) against another resident of England (Matusevitch), both of whom were Russian émigrés. The libel was first contained in a letter written by Matusevitch, which accused Telnikoff of being a racist hatemonger. Later the comments were published in an English newspaper. The court in *Telnikoff* refused to enforce the English judgment because it found that Maryland and English defamation law were rooted in fundamental public policy differences concerning the First Amendment's protection for freedom of the press and speech. Even if one accepts the point that the differences in the libel laws of England and the United States are such that they meet the very high bar that is usually required to satisfy the "public policy" exception, there is a more serious objection here. The question to be asked is: when does a country itself have interests that are sufficiently implicated to warrant application of its own public policy? Let me elaborate further. In *Telnikoff*, neither of the parties nor the transaction had any connection to the United States at the time of the transaction or the proceedings in England. The only nexus with the United States was the fact that the judgment debtor eventually moved to the United States and had assets there.

One can imagine a finite number of situations where there would be an international consensus about norms that would deem recognition or enforcement of a judgment to violate public policy without looking to any territorial nexus. However, in a case like *Telnikoff*, what is at stake are differing English and American views about the appropriate balance between protection of reputation and free speech. And in the *Telnikoff* example, it is England that has the relevant policy interests with respect to these parties and the transaction in question. In a traditional conflict-of-laws analysis, the United States would have "no interest" in applying its standards of behavior and recovery to these parties. Therefore, it seems inappropriate for U.S. standards to be invoked as a public policy defense in a recognition /enforcement context. That view was expressed by the dissenting judge in the *Telnikoff* case who concluded his dissent with the following observation:

> Public policy should not require us to give First Amendment protection . . . to English residents in publications distributed only in England. Failure to make our constitutional provisions relating to defamation applicable to wholly internal English defamation would not seem to violate fundamental notions of what is decent and just and should not undermine public confidence in the administration of law. The Court does little or no analysis of the global public policy considerations and seems inclined to make Maryland libel law applicable to the rest of the world by providing a safe haven for foreign libel judgment debtors.[11]

The interests of the United States with respect to recognition and enforcement are far different where a U.S. party publishes in the United States and distributes a work both in the United States and abroad and then is sued in a foreign jurisdiction for libel under the more stringent defamation laws of that country. In such a case, both the foreign jurisdiction and the United States would seem to want their respective policies applied, but the United States would be justified in concluding that its First Amendment concerns should lead to non-recognition of a judgment if the rendering court did apply foreign law. There could be disagreement on this point because principles of comity have generally led courts in the United States to enforce foreign country *judgments* in situations where they would *apply a different law* were the case brought in a U.S. court in the first instance. But in the above hypothetical, invocation of the public policy exception would probably be appropriate at the recognition/enforcement stage, if the foreign judgment substantially undermined protective speech in the United States.[12] There are other cases that are more complicated. For example, if a U.S party directly and intentionally publishes and distributes material solely in a foreign country, that country may have the stronger interest in having its own law applied, and the U.S. should, in the interests of comity, enforce that judgment.[13]

I do not take a firm position with respect to whether the judgments described in any of these last examples should be enforced, but they illustrate my point that H.R. 6146 fails to contain any nuance for these private international law concerns. The bill may encourage U.S. courts to apply U.S. law principles without regard to context and to invoke public policy too reflexively without sufficient regard for the competing interests of other countries. The danger is then that this provision will invite "libel tourism" in reverse -- where courts in the United States impose the United States view of free speech on the rest of the world regardless of the particular circumstances. The United States would then be engaging in the precise behavior of which it has been so critical.

I do believe that if the federal legislation were better able to articulate a nuanced and uniform national standard – thus offering the possibility of Supreme Court superintendence of such a standard – it would be preferable to the patchwork of solutions that are likely to be created at the state level.[14] But I return to the point I made at the outset of my remarks – the need generally for a broader solution on the national, indeed the international level, and one that belongs in the hands of Congress.

Let me offer an example of why a more comprehensive approach to recognition and enforcement of foreign judgments is desirable. There are other defenses that might be asserted to refuse recognition and enforcement of these "libel tourism" judgments that would take account of the jurisdictional excesses of foreign courts. When a foreign court exercises jurisdiction over a U.S. defendant in what might be regarded as an exorbitant assertion of jurisdiction (in a defamation case or any other), generally accepted principles of law in the United States relating to the recognition and enforcement of foreign judgments provide that such a judgment should not be recognized or enforced.[15] Thus, it is not only the defense of "public policy" but also the defense of an "unreasonable assertion of jurisdiction" that might be used to prevent recognition and enforcement of a foreign defamation judgment that is thought to undermine fundamental U.S. interests. However, H.R. 6146 concerns itself with only a very small piece of the more general problem of recognition and enforcement of foreign country judgments and does not address other relevant aspects.

As you might expect from my earlier comments, I am highly critical of the attempts made in H.R. 5814 and S. 2977 to authorize jurisdiction and to create a cause of action for a declaratory judgment and other relief on behalf of "any United States person" who is sued for defamation in a foreign country if such speech or writing by that person "has been published, uttered, or otherwise disseminated in the United States." As I indicated above, the attempt to impose the standards of U.S. defamation law on the rest of the world goes too far in many situations, and the reach of this provision fails to give proper respect to the interests of other countries. The jurisdiction provision in the bills that purports to assert jurisdiction over any person who has brought a foreign lawsuit against a "U.S. person" (when speech has also been published or disseminated in the United States) is constitutionally problematic under the Due Process Clause of the Fifth Amendment. A person who brings a lawsuit in a foreign country and serves a defendant in the United States does not engage in the kind of "purposeful conduct" directed to the United States that the Supreme Court has required to meet the constitutional standard of "minimum contacts" and "reasonableness" for asserting jurisdiction.[16] Finally, in addition to the remedy of a declaratory judgment provided by H.R. 5814 and S. 2977, these bills offer more extreme and ultimately unsustainable remedies -- a "clawback" of damages recovered in the foreign judgment, an anti-suit injunction, and an award of treble damages in certain circumstances. These tools are much too aggressive an assertion of U.S. jurisdiction even in those situations where U.S. interests might be found to be compelling. One need only be reminded of the possibility that an anti-suit injunction by a court in the United States may meet with the response of an anti-anti-suit injunction in the foreign court to realize that accommodation of competing policies is best achieved in other ways.[17]

One should not assume that other countries are oblivious to the concerns of the United States with respect to global defamation. Where the interests of the foreign country are minimal, we have seen foreign courts abstain and/or refuse jurisdiction to hear a libel case against a U.S.-based publisher.[18] Also, recent developments in Europe, such as the European Convention on Human Rights and the International Covenant of Civil and Political Rights are having an impact on the libel laws of many countries, including England,[19] and may result in greater sensitivity to principles akin to the First Amendment.[20]

I believe a comprehensive federal statute is the best solution to address the important and complex issues relating to the recognition and enforcement of foreign country judgments, including the particular issue of interest to this Committee – the problem of "libel tourism". It may well be that even national law will fall short in dealing with the problems arising from transnational libels and that only an international solution can ultimately address an issue that has become as global as the Internet itself. [21] But to the extent that Congress seeks a solution, it should do so by developing a broader proposal for federal law on the recognition and enforcement of foreign judgments and viewing the issues in the context of the foreign relations concerns of which they are a part.

End Notes

[1] See Hilton v. Guyot, 159 U.S. 113 (1895).

[2] For a more extensive explanation of how state law became the source of law for the recognition and enforcement of foreign country judgments with a critique of why the question should be viewed as a matter of federal law and national concern, see American Law Institute, Recognition and Enforcement of Foreign Judgments: Analysis and Proposed Federal Statute 1-6 (2006)(Hereinafter "ALI Proposed Federal Statute").

[3] As of 2008, the 1962 version of the Uniform Act – the Uniform Foreign Money-Judgments Recognition Act—is in effect in 30 states and territories of the United States. See Uniform Foreign Money-Judgments Recognition Act (1962), 13 Uniform Laws Annotated Part II (2002 ed. and 2008 Supp.). In 2005, the National Conference of Commissioners of Uniform State Law (NCCUSL) promulgated a revised Act – the Uniform Foreign-Country Money Judgments Recognition Act – that made slight changes to the earlier Act. See 13 Uniform Laws Annotated Part II (2008 Supp). The 2005 Act replaced the earlier 1962 Act in four states (California, Colorado, Idaho, and Michigan) and was adopted by another (Nevada). See http://www.nccusl.org/Update/uniformact_factsheets/uniformacts-fs-ufcmjra.asp. A number of other states have introduced bills to adopt the Revised Act.

[4] The prevailing judgment plaintiff attempted to enforce an English libel judgment in the United States in Telnikoff v. Matusevitch, 347 Md. 561, 792 A.2d 230 (Md. Ct. App. 1997)(on certified question from D.C. Circuit).

[5] This was the situation in Yahoo! Inc. v. La Ligue Contre Le Racisme, 433 F.3d 1199 (9th Cir. 2006)(en banc) and Ehrenfeld v. Bin Mahfouz, 518 F.3d 102 (2d Cir. 2008). In both cases, the actions for declaratory judgment were dismissed. In *Yahoo*, a combination of lack of ripeness and lack of jurisdiction led to the dismissal. In *Ehrenfeld*, the case was dismissed for lack of jurisdiction over the foreign judgment plaintiff.

[6] See Linda J. Silberman, Some Judgements on Judgments: A View from America, [2008] 19 King's Law Journal 235, 244-48.

98   Linda J. Silberman

[7] There can be different formulations of the "public policy" defense. For example, the 1962 Uniform Act (§ 4(b)(3)) provides that a judgment need not be recognized if the "cause of action"[claim for relief] on which the judgment is based is repugnant to the public policy of this state." The 2005 Revised Act reads slightly different; it provides that a foreign-county judgment need not be recognized if "the *judgment* or the [cause of action][claim for relief] on which the judgment is based is repugnant to the *public policy of this state or of the United States*." (Emphasis added). The ALI Proposed Federal Statute provides that "a foreign judgment shall not be enforced in a court in the United States if the party resisting recognition or enforcement establishes that . . . *the judgment or the claim on which the judgment is based* is repugnant to the *public policy of the United States*, or to the *public policy of a particular state of the United States when the relevant legal interest, right, or policy is regulated by state law*." (Emphasis added).

[8] See, e.g., Sarl Louis Feraud International v. Viewfinder, Inc., 489 F.3d 474 (2d Cir. 2007); Telnikoff v. Matusevitch, 347 Md. 561, 792 A.2d 250 (Md.Ct.App. 1997)(on certified question from D.C. Circuit); Bachchan v. India Abroad Publications, 585 N.Y.S. 2d 661 (Sup.Ct. N.Y. 1992).

[9] The certified question to the Maryland Court of Appeals from the Court of Appeals of the District of Columbia Circuit in Telnikoff v. Matusevitch, 347 Md. 561, 702 A.2d 230 (Md. Ct. App. 1997) was "whether recognition of an English libel judgment would be repugnant to *the public policy of Maryland.*" (Emphasis added). In *Telnikoff*, the parties agreed in oral argument that they viewed the case as being controlled by the First Amendment. In resting its decision on Maryland public policy as it was required to do under the Maryland certification legislation, the Maryland Court of Appeals observed that it was "appropriate to examine and rely upon the history, policies, and requirements of the First Amendment." The question of "federal" or "state" policy was potentially relevant because Maryland public policy arguably protected defamation even where the First Amendment did not. But the public policy relating to the First Amendment should be national public policy, and state public policy should be subordinated to national policy in a case such as this. For more on the proper relationship between state and federal policy in the context of a federal standard for recognition and enforcement of foreign judgments, see ALI Proposed Federal Statute § 5(a)(vi) and comment *h*, at 62-64.

[10] 347 Md. 561, 702 A.2d 230 (Md.Ct.App. 1997).

[11] Telnikoff v. Matusevitch, 347 Md. 561, 621-22, 702 A.2d 230, 250-51 (Md. Ct. App. 1997)(Chasanow, J., dissenting).

[12] Bachchan v. India Abroad Publications, 585 N.Y.S. 2d 661 (N.Y.Sup.Ct. 1992) is a slight variation. In *Bachchan*, an Indian plaintiff brought suit in England against a foreign news agency operating in New York and elsewhere that had distributed a news story about misconduct in India that was carried in both England and New York. The New York state trial court refused to enforce the English libel judgment on the ground that enforcement of the judgment would violate the First Amendment. There are differences of view here with respect to the propriety of invoking the public policy exception in these circumstances. Compare Kyu Ho Youm, Suing American Media in Foreign Courts: Doing an End-Run Around U.S. Libel Law, 16 Hastings Comm. & Ent. L.J. 235 (1994)(pointing out that U.S. libel law offers publishers significantly more protections than does English law) with Craig A. Stern, Foreign Judgments and the Freedom of Speech: Look Who's Talking, 60 Brook. L. Rev. 999, 1033-34 (1994)(criticizing *Bachchan* because England had the relevant interest in applying its law of defamation to this case).

[13] Cf. Desai v. Hersh, 719 F. Supp. 670 (N.D. Ill. 1989), aff'd, 954 F.2d 1408 (1992).

[14] Two states, New York and Illinois, have passed their own "libel tourism" laws. In 2008 New York amended its version of the Uniform Act to provide that a defamation judgment obtained outside of the United States need not be enforced unless the court in New York determines that the defamation law applied by the foreign court provides "at least as much protection for freedom of speech and press . . . as would be provided by both the United

States and New York Constitutions." CPLR §5304(b)(8)(2008). In addition, New York amended its jurisdictional statute, CPLR §302(a), to provide that any person who obtains a judgment in a defamation proceeding outside the United States against a New York resident or person amenable to jurisdiction in New York with assets in New York is subject to jurisdiction in New York for the purpose of obtaining declaratory relief, provided the alleged defamatory publication was made in New York and the person against whom the judgment was rendered has assets in New York or may have to take action in New York to comply with the judgment. Illinois amended its version of the Uniform Foreign Money-Judgments Recognition Act to add an additional ground for non-enforcement: "when the cause of action resulted in a defamation judgment obtained in a jurisdiction outside the United States, unless a court sitting in this State first determines that the defamation law applied in the foreign jurisdiction provides at least as much protection for freedom of speech and the press as provided for by both the United States and Illinois Constitutions." 735 ILCS 5/12-621(b)(7)(2009). Illinois also amended its jurisdictional statute to allow for jurisdiction over Illinois residents for the purpose of rendering declaratory relief provided the publication was published in Illinois and the resident has assets in Illinois to satisfy the judgment or may have to take action in Illinois to comply with the judgment. 735 ILCS 5/2-209(b)(5)(2009).

[15] See, e.g., Uniform Foreign Money-Judgments Recognition Act § 4(a)(2).

[16] See Asahi Metal Industry Co., Ltd. v. Superior Court, 480 U.S. 102 (1987).

[17] See Andreas F. Lowenfeld, Forum Shopping Antisuit Injunctions, Negative Declarations, and Related Tools of International Litigation, 91 Am J. Int'l L. 314 (1997).

[18] See Jameel v. Dow Jones & Co., Inc., [2005] EWCA (Civ) 75 (staying libel action brought by Saudi claimants against the U.S.-based Dow Jones where only 5 subscribers in England had accessed the hyperlink disclosing claimants' names); Bangoura v. Washington Post [2005] D.L.R. (4th) 341 (holding that Ontario trial court could not exercise jurisdiction over Washington Post for allegedly libelous statements posted on its website where plaintiff was not an Ontario resident at the time the article was written).

[19] See, e.g., the recent decision of the House of Lords, Jameel v. Wall Street Journal Europe [2006]UKHL 44, [2007] 1 A.C. 359 (Eng.), which has been characterized as "moving English defamation law much closer to the American constitutional law of defamation"). See Marin Roger Scordato, The International Legal Environment for Serious Political Reporting Has Fundamentally Changed: Understanding the Revolutionary New Era of English Defamation Law, 40 Conn. L. Rev. 165 (2007).

[20] See generally Michael Traynor, Conflict of Laws, Comparative Law, and The American Law Institute, 49 Am J. Comp. L. 391, 396 (2001).

[21] See Dow Jones & Co., Inc. v. Gutnick [2002]HCA 56 (Dec. 10 2002)(Australia)(Referring to the problems of the publication of defamatory material on the internet, Justice Kirby of the Australian High Court observed that the problems "appear to warrant national legislative attention and to require international discussion in a forum as global as the Internet itself.").

In: Libel Tourism and Foreign Libel Lawsuits
Editor: Amy J. Brower

ISBN: 978-1-61209-148-8
© 2011 Nova Science Publishers, Inc.

Chapter 7

TESTIMONY OF KURT WIMMER, PARTNER, COVINGTON & BURLING LLP, HEARING ON "ARE FOREIGN LIBEL LAWSUITS CHILLING AMERICANS' FIRST AMENDMENT RIGHTS?"

Chairman Leahy, Ranking Member Sessions, and Members of the Committee, thank you for inviting me here this morning, and thank you for addressing this issue today.

For the past 15 years, I have been advising publishers, authors and technology companies on how to continue to publish the robust news and information that Americans deserve, and that our First Amendment protects, in an era when publishers can be sued in foreign jurisdictions that do not protect free expression simply because their work can be accessed through the Internet. The issues you are addressing today can help to preserve the vitality of the First Amendment in an internationally networked world.

In countries quite literally from A to Z — from Australia to Zimbabwe — courts, litigants and prosecutors have pursued distant authors based on Internet publications intended for the authors' local readers. From my vantage point, it seems clear that the potential for being sued or prosecuted on the basis of an online publication does, in fact, chill the exercise of essential First Amendment freedoms. This chill can result in self-censorship, in decisions not to publish, and in decisions to review and assess American content based on legal standards that are less protective of free expression than our laws. This chilling effect can undermine the search for truth that our First Amendment demands, in areas that are as essential to our national security as terrorism. As

Senator Specter has said, "freedom of expression of ideas, opinions, and research, and freedom of exchange of information are all essential to the functioning of a democracy, and the fight against terrorism." That freedom is endangered by libel tourism.

Some ask whether publication of sensitive matters really would be chilled, given that U.S. courts have refused to enforce judgments rendered by foreign courts applying laws that do not comply with our constitutional standards. In Bachchan v. India Abroad Publications Inc., for example, a New York state trial court noted that England lacks an equivalent to the First Amendment and concluded "[t]he protection to free speech and the press embodied in that amendment would be seriously jeopardized by the entry of foreign libel judgments granted pursuant to standards deemed appropriate in England but considered antithetical to the protections afforded the press by the U.S. Constitution." Given this view, shouldn't U.S. authors publish to the world just as they publish to America, and simply rely on U.S. courts to refuse to enforce any foreign judgments that result?

The answer, sadly, is that the very act of rendering a foreign judgment has immediate and damaging effects on the publisher or author who is sued, before a judgment is ever enforced – and, in many cases, even if it is never enforced. The impact of the sword of Damocles is not that it falls, but that it hangs.

The United Nations Human Rights Committee has recognized these same chilling effects. In a 2008 Report, the Human Rights Committee expressed its concern that the United Kingdom's "practical application of the law of libel has served to discourage critical media reporting on matters of serious public interest, adversely affecting the ability of scholars and journalists to publish their work, including through the phenomenon known as 'libel tourism.'" The Human Rights Committee further noted the "advent of the internet and the international distribution of foreign media also create the danger that a State party's unduly restrictive libel law will affect freedom of expression worldwide on matters of valid public interest."

Just as in all First Amendment analysis, proving a chill is a challenge. We cannot know for certain when punches have been pulled, when stories have been killed, and when manuscripts have been left unpublished. There are, however, a few concrete examples.

In 2006, the Cambridge University Press, surely one of the most prestigious and well-funded publishers in the world, received a libel claim for a book by American professor Robert Collins and former State Department official J. Millard Burr entitled Alms for Jihad: Charity and Terrorism in the Islamic World. The libel plaintiff was a Saudi billionaire, Sheik Khalid bin

Mahfouz, who claimed the book defamed him by linking him to the funding of terrorism. Rather than mount a spirited defense, Cambridge University Press folded and settled with Sheik bin Mahfouz — it simply couldn't afford the litigation. In 2007, it not only ceased publishing the book, but shredded all unsold copies. It asked all libraries that had purchased the book to destroy it. The American Library Association advised libraries not to pulp the book. "Unless there is an order from a U.S. court, the British settlement is unenforceable in the United States, and libraries are under no legal obligation to return or destroy the book," its Office of Intellectual Freedom stated in a release. "Given the intense interest in the book, and the desire of readers to learn about the controversy firsthand, we recommend that U.S. libraries keep the book available for their users." If even the Cambridge University Press cannot stand up to well-financed libel tourists, how can other publishers truly be expected to do so?

The National Endowment for Democracy's Center for International Media Assistance published just last month an excellent report entitled Libel Tourism: Silencing the Press Through Transnational Legal Threats. In the report, investigative journalist Drew Sullivan traces the chilling effect of transborder libel litigation around the world, and the examples of investigative journalists buckling under the pressure of litigation are telling.

There is no doubt that even foreign defamation judgments that are not enforced can cause real damage to U.S. authors who are sued abroad. The Ehrenfeld v. bin Mahfouz case is illustrative.

The same billionaire who conquered the Cambridge University Press and sued almost 40 other publishers, Sheik bin Mahfouz, obtained a default judgment against Dr. Rachel Ehrenfeld in the United Kingdom, including damages, legal fees, a "declaration of falsity," an order directing Dr. Ehrenfeld and her publisher to publish an apology, and an injunction against the further publication of the challenged statements. This foreign judgment may impede Dr. Ehrenfeld from obtaining future publishing contracts, as publishers typically carry insurance policies requiring them to review the liability risks of works they consider for publication, and they may shy away from an author subject to such a foreign judgment. Dr. Ehrenfeld told a New York court that publishers who accepted her work in the past declined to do so after the English judgment.

Foreign libel judgments, especially those accompanied by a "declaration of falsity," also impose reputational harms on authors and publishers. No author or publisher wants to be tarred with the brush of a defamation judgment. This is especially true if that judgment states that the author or publisher published statements deemed by a court to be untrue. Unless a United States author is provided with a mechanism to challenge the foreign judgment on his or her own initiative, the foreign libel plaintiff can deprive the author or publisher with an opportunity to vindicate his or her reputation.

These chilling effects are not merely side effects of a foreign defamation judgment. Instead, they may be the prime motivation for filing suit in a foreign country with lesser protections for freedom of expression. Again, the Ehrenfeld case is illustrative. When he sued Dr. Ehrenfeld, Sheik bin Mahfouz was a financier and billionaire with business interests around the world. The money judgment he obtained in his English lawsuit against Dr. Ehrenfeld, although a huge burden for Dr. Ehrenfeld, would be less than rounding error to a man of Sheik bin Mahfouz's staggering wealth. Instead, the greatest benefits of this judgment to a plaintiff such as Sheik bin Mahfouz are the English court's "declaration of falsity" and injunction.

Indeed, a foreign libel plaintiff may never seek enforcement of the judgment obtained in the foreign court, especially if the plaintiff knows that a United States court will refuse to enforce it. Instead, the libel plaintiff simply wants to use it to chill criticism. For example, Sheik bin Mahfouz took no action to enforce the default judgment he obtained against Dr. Ehrenfeld (but refused to disclaim is his right to enforce it in the future) and maintains a website where he has posted information about the suit he brought against her and suits he has brought against other authors and publishers. The website also contains a warning designed to chill future criticism of him: "Khalid bin Mahfouz and his family reserve their rights against the authors, editors, publishers, distributors and printers of these publications [and] they expressly reserve their rights against any person or entity which repeats any of the erroneous allegations contained in these or any other publications."

This chilling effect not only jeopardizes individual members of the media, but also impedes the crucial free flow of information and ideas to the American public on matters of public concern. Foreign litigation against United States publications and authors constitutes a clear threat to the ability of the American press to vigorously investigate and publish news and information about the most crucial issues before the American public. If a member of the media may be sued in any country in which a handful of individuals have accessed or purchased a work, the media loses the important ability to predict which country's laws will apply to the work. In such a situation, an author or publisher may have no choice but to tailor the work to the standards of the nations that afford the weakest protections for free expression. It will not matter than the speech being curtailed would be protected in the United States.

This chill damages not only the free flow of protected speech to Americans. If the process continues and publishers continue to take efforts to limit the ability of their speech to be accessed outside of the United States, the rest of the world will no longer have access to the robust American investigative journalism that often is the only light being shed on despotic regimes and corrupt governments.

Under current law, most American authors and publishers must wait for the foreign plaintiff to take action enforcing the judgment in the United States. This limitation permits the foreign plaintiff to use that foreign judgment to chill future criticism while also ensuring that a United States court will not have jurisdiction over him to declare the judgment unenforceable. Some American authors in now have the right to bring actions in state courts, thanks to statutes adopted by a few states in the past two years. But this is a national – indeed international – problem that calls out for a national solution.

Will legislation within the United States solve this problem entirely? To be sure, it would only be a step. International law reform also will be essential, and the process of obtaining that reform will be a significant project (which I describe in an article that I have submitted for the record). This Committee can move this law-reform process ahead by continuing to focus on this issue, and to consider meaningful legislation that will permit U.S. authors, journalists and publishers to take positive action to ameliorate some of the most damaging aspects of having to deal with foreign litigants. It is an essential first step, and I am gratified that the Committee is considering it.

Thank you again for your time today, and I would be pleased to respond to any questions you have.

CHAPTER SOURCES

The following chapters have been previously published:

Chapter 1 – This is an edited, excerpted and augmented edition of a United States Congressional Research Service publication, Report Order Code R40497, dated March 5, 2010.

Chapter 2 – This is an edited, excerpted and augmented edition of a United States Congressional Research Service publication, Report Order Code R41417, dated September 16, 2010.

Chapter 3 – These remarks were delivered as Testimony of Dr. Rachel Ehrenfeld, before the House Committee on the Judiciary Hearing on Libel Tourism, given February 12, 2009.

Chapter 4 – These remarks were delivered as Testimony of Bruce D. Brown, before the House Committee on the Judiciary Hearing on Libel Tourism, given February 12, 2009.

Chapter 5 – These remarks were delivered as Testimony of Laura R. Handman, before the House Committee on the Judiciary Hearing on Libel Tourism, given February 12, 2009.

Chapter 6 – These remarks were delivered as Statement of Professor Linda J. Silberman, before the House Committee on the Judiciary Hearing on Libel Tourism, given February 12, 2009.

Chapter 7 – These remarks were delivered as Testimony of Kurt Wimmer, before the House Committee on the Judiciary Hearing on Libel Tourism, given February 23, 2010.

INDEX

9

9/11, vii, 17, 49

A

access, viii, 22, 43, 72, 77, 88, 105
accommodation, 96
agencies, 50, 53, 75
airplane, 50
ALI, 88, 91, 97, 98
antitrust, 17, 38, 46, 47
arms sales, 50, 80
articulation, 21, 43
assault, 65, 79, 87
assets, 3, 7, 14, 15, 16, 18, 29, 32, 35, 44,
    52, 84, 94, 99
authority, 2, 10, 24, 38, 46, 47, 79

B

banking, 51, 53
benefits, 12, 62, 104
blood, 65, 72, 81
Britain, viii, 21, 31, 41, 52, 56, 58, 60, 65,
    68, 75, 76, 77, 78, 79, 84, 87
businesses, 53

C

case law, 5, 16

censorship, 52, 65, 79, 101
certification, 98
challenges, 53
charities, 51, 61
children, 61
CIA, 53
circulation, 78
citizens, vii, 1, 45, 53
City, viii, 72
civil rights, 81
clarity, 5, 30, 75
clients, viii, 55, 59, 63, 71
commercial, 69
common law, 3, 5, 6, 8, 19, 20, 21, 28, 29,
    30, 33, 40, 41, 43, 80
communication, 6, 30, 41
Communications Act, vii, 27, 29, 36, 45
Communications Act of 1934, vii, 27, 29,
    36, 45
Communications Decency Act, 73, 87
community, 75
competing interests, 95
competitors, 59
computer, 36, 45
conflict, 37, 45, 94
Congress, iv, vii, 2, 7, 14, 15, 16, 20, 21, 24,
    27, 35, 37, 38, 39, 40, 41, 45, 46, 50, 53,
    66, 79, 84, 86, 92, 95, 97
Constitution, vii, 1, 5, 7, 9, 10, 16, 18, 20,
    27, 29, 32, 34, 36, 37, 38, 39, 40, 44, 46,
    53, 74, 79, 81, 82, 93, 102

Index

constitutional law, 67, 79, 99
constitutional limitations, 50
constitutional principles, 37
controversial, 58, 63
corruption, 51, 53, 72
cost, 10, 58, 65, 76
Council of Europe, 19, 40, 50
counseling, viii, 71
Court of Appeals, 12, 44, 64, 81, 82, 98
court proceedings, 36
covering, 55
criticism, 50, 62, 75, 104, 105
critics, 6, 30, 52, 69

D

damages, iv, 1, 2, 4, 5, 6, 8, 9, 12, 15, 18, 23, 30, 31, 33, 44, 45, 58, 61, 66, 67, 74, 75, 78, 84, 86, 96, 103, 105
danger, 95, 102
defamation, vii, 1, 3, 4, 5, 6, 13, 14, 15, 17, 19, 20, 22, 24, 27, 28, 29, 30, 34, 35, 36, 37, 39, 40, 43, 44, 46, 58, 63, 65, 66, 75, 77, 78, 83, 86, 87, 88, 93, 94, 95, 96, 98, 99, 103, 104
defendants, 1, 2, 3, 4, 6, 7, 10, 14, 16, 17, 18, 22, 23, 24, 29, 30, 31, 32, 35, 41, 44, 51, 57, 60, 62, 65, 68, 74, 77, 79
democracy, 2, 4, 20, 32, 42, 50, 53, 102
Denmark, 59
depth, 21, 41
destination, 19, 29, 40, 68, 87
diamonds, 65
diplomatic efforts, 38, 39
distribution, 63, 80, 102
District of Columbia, 71, 98
diversity, 36
drawing, 58
drug trade, 50
drug trafficking, 50
due process, 10, 11, 16, 22, 35, 36, 39, 44, 60, 66, 85

E

economic resources, 52

electronic communications, 83
employees, 41
employment, 15, 72
enemies, 50
enforcement, vii, viii, 2, 7, 9, 13, 14, 15, 16, 17, 22, 24, 27, 28, 32, 34, 35, 36, 38, 39, 42, 44, 45, 52, 66, 73, 75, 79, 80, 83, 84, 85, 88, 89, 91, 92, 93, 94, 95, 97, 98, 99, 104
England, vii, viii, 1, 3, 4, 5, 6, 7, 8, 18, 19, 20, 25, 28, 29, 30, 31, 32, 40, 42, 51, 55, 57, 58, 59, 60, 61, 63, 72, 73, 74, 75, 76, 77, 78, 79, 80, 81, 82, 84, 87, 93, 94, 97, 98, 99, 102
enlargement, 83
environment, 87
equilibrium, 66
Europe, 19, 40, 41, 50, 52, 75, 81, 86, 97, 99
European Community, 47, 52
European Union, 42
evidence, viii, 15, 22, 37, 41, 46, 47, 50, 53, 55, 57, 58, 59, 67, 75
execution, 15, 16, 64
exercise, 9, 10, 11, 12, 22, 23, 35, 36, 38, 44, 76, 99, 101
exile, 56
experiences, 63
exposure, 4, 31, 63, 87

F

fairness, 35, 76
faith, viii, 16, 21, 24, 41, 42, 76, 80, 92
families, 61, 72
family members, 57
fear, viii, 2, 4, 56, 64
federal courts, 10, 11, 13, 16, 21, 22, 23, 34, 35, 37, 38, 39, 43, 55, 66
federal law, 7, 14, 29, 32, 37, 45, 46, 79, 97
Federal Rules of Civil Procedure, 11, 17
federal statute, 2, 10, 15, 37, 44, 88, 91, 92, 97
federalism, 38
Fifth Amendment, 10, 96
financial, 15, 59

Index

financial support, 15

First Amendment, vi, viii, ix, 1, 3, 4, 5, 15, 17, 18, 19, 20, 22, 24, 25, 28, 29, 36, 38, 39, 40, 42, 43, 45, 49, 50, 52, 55, 56, 62, 63, 64, 66, 69, 72, 73, 74, 79, 80, 81, 82, 84, 86, 88, 89, 92, 93, 94, 95, 97, 98, 101, 102

food, 50

force, 42, 45, 53, 88

foreign affairs, 24, 38, 46

formation, 61

forum non conveniens, 4, 31, 60, 68

Fourteenth Amendment, 6, 10, 22, 30, 44

France, 12, 44, 78

fraud, 8, 33

freedom, vii, 5, 13, 17, 19, 20, 21, 22, 30, 34, 38, 40, 41, 42, 43, 44, 49, 50, 53, 56, 65, 79, 87, 93, 99, 102, 104

freedom of expression, 19, 40, 79, 102, 104

Full Faith and Credit clause, 7, 16

funding, 5, 15, 103

funds, 51, 53, 61

G

Georgia, 88

Gertz v. Robert Welch, 6, 30, 68, 75

governments, 53, 105

governor, 88

Great Britain, 76, 77

H

Hamas, 51, 61, 62

harbors, 74

harmonization, 46

Hawaii, 88

heroin, 50

Hezbollah, 51, 62

Hilton v. Guyot, 7, 21, 32, 42, 88, 97

history, ix, 3, 27, 28, 37, 39, 45, 47, 56, 64, 92, 98

hostility, 21, 41

House, 2, 3, 5, 7, 18, 19, 28, 31, 35, 37, 40, 42, 50, 64, 75, 78, 79, 83, 84, 88, 99, 107

House of Commons, 2, 3, 7, 18, 28, 79

House of Representatives, 84

I

Iceland, 59

immunity, 6, 20, 30, 40, 50, 76

impacts, 5, 63

inadmissible, 51

independence, 53, 56

India, 22, 43, 56, 72, 80, 81, 82, 86, 88, 98, 102

Indians, 80

individuals, 6, 20, 30, 42, 77, 104

industry, 50, 57, 66

injuries, 3, 28

injury, iv, 23, 67

international law, 46, 93, 95

international relations, 2, 16, 18

international terrorism, 53, 62

Internet, vii, ix, 4, 7, 22, 31, 43, 49, 51, 58, 59, 60, 65, 76, 78, 79, 83, 87, 97, 99, 101

intervention, 66

intimidation, 20

investment, 59

investment bank, 59

Ireland, 77, 84

Islam, 63

issues, viii, ix, 2, 6, 15, 20, 41, 49, 61, 71, 75, 97, 101, 104

J

jihad, 65

journalism, 6, 7, 21, 30, 41, 55, 63, 64, 65, 75, 105

journalists, 50, 73, 76, 102, 103, 105

judiciary, 19, 24, 42, 45

Judiciary Committee, 5, 19, 31, 37, 42

jurisdiction, vii, 2, 3, 4, 9, 10, 11, 12, 13, 14, 15, 16, 19, 22, 23, 28, 29, 31, 34, 35, 36, 39, 40, 42, 44, 49, 51, 52, 59, 60, 66, 73, 76, 77, 82, 83, 84, 87, 88, 94, 95, 96, 97, 99, 105

K

kidnapping, 64

112 Index

knees, 61
Korea, 51
Kyrgyzstan, 87

L

law enforcement, 75
laws, iv, vii, ix, 1, 2, 3, 5, 7, 8, 9, 12, 16, 17, 18, 19, 21, 22, 24, 25, 27, 28, 29, 31, 33, 34, 36, 37, 38, 39, 40, 43, 49, 52, 53, 59, 60, 65, 66, 69, 73, 74, 75, 77, 78, 79, 82, 83, 84, 85, 87, 92, 94, 97, 98, 101, 102, 104
lawyers, viii, 63, 72, 79
lead, 51, 95
Leahy, 24, 101
learning, 64
legal issues, 2, 15
legislation, 16, 18, 37, 46, 56, 66, 73, 79, 83, 84, 85, 86, 95, 98, 105
legislative proposals, 2, 3, 5, 18
legislative responses, 2, 9
libel judgment, vii, 2, 3, 7, 9, 13, 15, 16, 17, 18, 22, 24, 27, 28, 32, 34, 37, 38, 39, 43, 72, 79, 80, 81, 82, 83, 84, 88, 89, 92, 93, 94, 97, 98, 102, 103
libel laws, iv, vii, 1, 2, 3, 7, 9, 18, 25, 27, 28, 31, 34, 49, 59, 65, 69, 73, 74, 75, 77, 78, 79, 82, 88, 94, 97
light, 15, 105
litigation, viii, 4, 7, 12, 15, 16, 20, 23, 31, 42, 52, 59, 66, 69, 71, 76, 103, 104
Louisiana, 88

M

magazines, viii, 71, 83
Maine, 88
majority, 22, 23, 31, 43, 52, 58
man, 19, 59, 104
marketplace, 20, 42
Maryland, 22, 43, 56, 72, 81, 82, 88, 93, 94, 98
matter, iv, ix, 8, 13, 16, 17, 32, 37, 41, 58, 60, 62, 67, 74, 75, 81, 84, 88, 92, 93, 97, 105

Matusevitch v. Telnikof, 81, 88
media, viii, 3, 7, 15, 30, 31, 52, 55, 60, 63, 66, 67, 71, 72, 73, 75, 77, 78, 81, 83, 84, 85, 86, 87, 102, 104
Mercury, 45
Mexico, 88
money laundering, 51, 53
Moscow, 59, 68
motivation, 7, 104
multiples, 84, 85

N

narcotics, 50
national policy, 98
national security, 2, 5, 31, 50, 53, 63, 101
negative effects, 15
Netherlands, 42
New York Times v. Sullivan, 1, 5, 20, 29, 41, 49, 65, 66
New Zealand, 87
nexus, 94
North Korea, 51
Northern Ireland, 77, 84

O

Obama, vii, 27
obstacles, 84
officials, 6, 20, 30, 40, 69
opportunities, 15

P

Pakistan, 20, 56, 57, 58, 64
Parliament, 6, 30, 53, 79, 87
participants, 63
peace, 7, 32
penalties, 3, 19, 28, 40
permit, 45, 66, 105
Philadelphia, 67, 86
playing, 79
policy, 5, 8, 9, 13, 18, 22, 23, 24, 31, 33, 34, 43, 44, 50, 72, 80, 81, 82, 93, 94, 95, 96, 98
policy makers, 50
precedent, 66, 72, 82

Index

113

predictability, 24, 38

prejudice, 8, 33

president, 62

President, vii, viii, 20, 27, 46, 56, 72, 78

prima facie, 22, 74, 79, 89

principles, 8, 24, 33, 37, 45, 75, 80, 81, 86, 92, 93, 95, 97

probability, 58, 69

procedural rule, 22

project, 64, 105

proposition, 57

prosecutors, 101

protection, 6, 13, 18, 19, 22, 30, 34, 36, 40, 41, 43, 44, 45, 50, 53, 63, 73, 74, 80, 83, 86, 93, 94, 99, 102

public concern, 1, 67, 72, 73, 74, 84, 86, 93, 104

public figures, 6, 30, 51, 57, 73, 75, 84

public interest, 7, 21, 30, 41, 62, 65, 68, 74, 75, 82, 102

public life, 6, 30

public officials, 6, 7, 30, 57, 75

public policy, 5, 8, 9, 13, 18, 22, 23, 24, 31, 33, 34, 43, 44, 50, 72, 80, 81, 82, 93, 94, 95, 96, 98

public support, 62

publishing, 59, 64, 68, 79, 80, 85, 103

pulp, 61, 88, 103

R

Rachel Ehrenfeld, v, 4, 19, 20, 31, 35, 41, 42, 49, 53, 59, 63, 78, 82, 103, 107

radio, 54, 72

ratification, 42

reading, 46

real estate, 69

reciprocity, ix, 8, 32, 42, 92

recognition, viii, 2, 7, 8, 9, 13, 16, 17, 18, 22, 23, 24, 32, 34, 36, 38, 39, 42, 43, 44, 79, 81, 82, 88, 91, 92, 93, 94, 95, 97, 98

recommendations, iv

recovery, 6, 20, 30, 40, 94

reform, 7, 18, 25, 31, 56, 65, 66, 69, 105

reforms, 2, 3, 18, 28, 65

regulations, 46

relief, 8, 14, 15, 22, 23, 33, 35, 51, 96, 98, 99

reporters, 18, 40, 63, 65, 82

repression, 51

Republican Party, 62

reputation, 19, 40, 56, 74, 94, 104

requirements, vii, 12, 16, 21, 23, 27, 29, 35, 36, 37, 39, 43, 66, 98

resources, 52, 60

response, 4, 17, 18, 29, 31, 42, 51, 52, 61, 65, 66, 72, 96

restrictions, 3, 19, 28, 37, 40, 46

retirement, 56

Reynolds Privilege, 6, 7, 21, 41

rights, iv, ix, 8, 9, 13, 15, 17, 23, 24, 33, 34, 38, 46, 52, 81, 86, 92, 104

risk, 52, 58, 63, 83

risks, viii, 64, 71, 103

rules, 2, 7, 22, 23, 32, 43, 62

Russia, 79

S

safe haven, 94

safety, 46

Saudi Arabia, 51

scholarship, 57

school, 55, 58

scope, 9, 31, 33, 37, 93

screening, 36

security, 2, 5, 31, 50, 53, 63, 101

separation of powers, 37

service provider, 22, 43, 76, 87

Sheikh Khalid Bin Mahfouz, 4, 31

showing, 21, 41, 57, 86, 89

side effects, 104

Singapore, 87

society, 50

solution, 92, 95, 97, 105

speech, 1, 3, 4, 5, 7, 13, 14, 15, 17, 18, 19, 20, 21, 22, 24, 28, 30, 31, 32, 34, 35, 38, 39, 40, 41, 43, 44, 52, 53, 56, 58, 63, 65, 66, 68, 76, 77, 80, 82, 83, 84, 85, 86, 92, 94, 95, 96, 99, 102, 105

SPEECH Act, v, vii, 27, 28, 29, 31, 34, 35, 36, 37, 38, 39, 45

114 Index

state, vii, viii, 2, 7, 8, 10, 11, 13, 15, 16, 17, 18, 21, 22, 23, 24, 27, 29, 32, 33, 34, 36, 37, 38, 39, 42, 43, 44, 45, 46, 53, 57, 66, 67, 76, 79, 80, 81, 82, 83, 84, 92, 93, 95, 97, 98, 102, 105
State Department, 102
state laws, ix, 2, 16, 22, 27, 36, 37, 39, 43, 66, 92
state legislatures, 8, 33
states, vii, ix, 2, 6, 7, 8, 9, 13, 16, 18, 19, 21, 22, 23, 24, 27, 30, 32, 33, 34, 36, 37, 40, 43, 44, 46, 50, 52, 61, 66, 67, 69, 79, 83, 85, 88, 92, 97, 98, 103, 105
statute of limitations, 7, 31, 76
statutes, vii, 2, 7, 8, 9, 13, 14, 15, 18, 21, 23, 27, 32, 33, 34, 35, 37, 43, 44, 45, 46, 47, 76, 85, 88, 105
streams, 19, 42
Supremacy Clause, 37
Supreme Court, ix, 1, 5, 6, 7, 8, 10, 11, 21, 22, 24, 29, 30, 32, 43, 44, 46, 49, 50, 66, 74, 75, 86, 92, 95, 96
Sweden, 80
Syria, 51

T

tactics, 59
target, 59
technology, ix, 101
tension, 58
territorial, 94
territory, 8, 33, 88
terrorism, 4, 5, 19, 20, 31, 40, 42, 50, 51, 53, 59, 61, 62, 63, 78, 84, 101, 103
terrorist groups, 18, 40, 60, 61
terrorist organization, 50, 51, 62
testing, 81
The New York Times, 54
threats, 23, 52, 77, 83
tracks, 44
trade, 50
traditions, 61
trafficking, 46, 50
training, 50
transformation, 66

translation, 60
Treasury, 53
treaties, 79
treatment, 6, 7, 32
trial, viii, 8, 33, 51, 57, 58, 71, 80, 88, 98, 99, 102

U

UK, 21, 41, 44, 87
Ukraine, 60
uniform, ix, 7, 8, 16, 21, 22, 23, 24, 27, 32, 33, 37, 39, 43, 44, 88, 92, 95
Uniform Foreign Money-Judgments Recognition Act, ix, 8, 33, 52, 92, 97, 99
Uniform Foreign-Country Money Judgments Recognition Act, 8, 33, 97
United, iv, viii, 1, 2, 3, 4, 6, 7, 9, 10, 11, 13, 14, 15, 16, 17, 18, 19, 20, 21, 22, 23, 24, 28, 29, 31, 32, 33, 34, 38, 39, 40, 41, 42, 43, 44, 46, 47, 50, 52, 71, 73, 74, 76, 77, 78, 79, 80, 81, 82, 83, 87, 88, 91, 92, 93, 94, 95, 96, 97, 98, 102, 103, 104, 105, 107
United Kingdom, 19, 21, 40, 42, 43, 46, 77, 83, 102, 103
United Nations, 102
United States, iv, viii, 1, 2, 3, 4, 6, 7, 9, 10, 11, 13, 14, 15, 16, 17, 18, 19, 20, 21, 22, 23, 24, 28, 29, 31, 32, 33, 34, 38, 39, 40, 41, 42, 43, 44, 46, 47, 50, 52, 71, 73, 74, 76, 77, 78, 79, 80, 81, 82, 83, 87, 88, 91, 92, 93, 94, 95, 96, 97, 98, 103, 104, 105, 107
universities, 64

V

vehicles, 50
venue, 3, 28
victims, 14, 52
video, 78
vision, 24
Volkswagen, 22, 44, 45
vote, 81
vulnerability, 66

Index

W

Wales, 77, 78
Washington, 21, 22, 41, 44, 45, 55, 58, 77, 81, 88, 99
web, 76, 84
websites, 23, 73, 76
World Bank, 56
worldwide, 83, 102

Y

Yahoo, 11, 12, 22, 43, 44, 88, 97
Yale University, 61

Z

Zimbabwe, 101